WARNOCK

UNCUT

A NOVEL BY

MICHAEL HIGGINS JR.

LAUGH THINK EAT
PRODUCTIONS

First Trade Paperback Edition Printing November 2017
1

MICHAEL HIGGINS JR® and LAUGH THINK EAT PRODUCTIONS® are Registered Trademark of AVIATION VIRTUES, LLC.

© 2018 by LAUGH THINK EAT PRODUCTIONS
www.LaughThinkEat.com

Library of Congress Control Number: 2017915666
ISBN: 978-0-692-78842-4
Author: MICHAEL HIGGINS JR
Cover Designer: Glenn Jones at www.wretchedgingerboy.com/

Printed in the United States of America

For information email WarnockUncut@outlook.com

WARNOCK

UNCUT

AUTHOR'S NOTES

Let me get straight to the point, this book is hilarious. Real rap, laugh out loud comedy is all over this jawn (If you don't know what jawn means, you'll be hip by the end of this jawn). Shiz, Jason, and Chico, are a great comedy threesome, like Martin, Tommy, and Cole.

On the flipside, don't be surprised if you feel inspired to improve yourself or chase your dreams by the end of this one of a kind novel. You will find wisdom and examples of how to gain an edge in business and in life throughout these pages. I know how to speak to the hopeless and bring them out of the cave of ignorance. I'm like the author version of Tupac Shakur, with the knowledge of self like Socrates.

PS: If you're not from Philly and your second oldest cousin wasn't stabbed or shot in Philly, go to the back of the book and read the Glossary (on page 188) first. I don't want you to have the huh face on, when you encounter words like jawn. Yes, jawn is a legit word in Philadelphia. So, if you don't know what jawn means, you need to read that jawn (the glossary), then dive in to this jawn (Warnock Uncut). PEACE!!!

This book is dedicated

To my nephews

D Nice & Scrap

MICHAEL HIGGINS JR.

PROLOGUE

On a clear summer afternoon, a prison guard, who favored Bill Goldberg, opened the entrance to Lewisburg Penitentiary. Charles Williams, AKA Chip, strolled away from his bondage, after eight years of enduring three hots and a cot. Chip's mahogany bald head reflected the sun's rays. Chiseled biceps and shoulders, made his throwback Randle Cunningham t-shirt, hug his muscular frame. Jailhouse rules were in full effect and Chip's black Guess jeans presented zero sagging. The white Air Force 1's on his feet embodied the 90's era in Philly. A blinding, VVS diamond pinky ring, left no question that the dope game was good to him before losing his freedom.

Before Chip could take two steps beyond his former bondage, the guard cut into him, "You were a Philadelphia drug lord, right?" A witty smirk came upon his face.

1

"Yea, I'm Richard Allen's finest," Chip's spoke in a smooth tone like Tyreese.

"On your way back, make sure to bring me a Philly cheesesteak from Pat's." The guard looked forward to Chip's down fall, because it was good for business.

A chipped tooth smile was presented by Chip, then he tranquilly replied, "I'm from North Philly, where Maxx's on Erie Ave is king. But I wouldn't suggest you go there for two reasons."

The guard folded his arms. "Why's that Chief?"

"For one, your green ass would look stupid asking for a Philly cheesesteak in Philadelphia. We just call them cheesesteaks. The last, and most important reason, why I wouldn't suggest you head to Maxx's, is the fact that some of the other brothers you pulled that corny joke on, hang around Maxx's. And I'm sure, it would be their pleasure to run your pockets or worse."

Before the guard could respond, Chip was on his way to the parking lot. He halted his progress when he spotted Cherie, standing on the sidewalk, next to her black 1995 Bonneville. His ride or die chick resembled Nina Long from Love Jones, with a white sundress hugging her petite frame. Dark chocolate full lips, glazed in Mac Lip Gloss, triggered blood to rush below Chip's belt. He envisioned pulling her Robust dreadlocks while letting his inner beast go buck wild. After speed walking to his desire, he wrapped her in his arms.

Cherie was overwhelmed in his embrace and breathtaking lip locking. If Chip was a clock, his manhood would be on three o'clock.

After being jabbed in the stomach, by eight inches of fresh out wood, Cherie stepped back and admired his timber. "Boy, do something with that, before we both get charged with indecent exposure."

Without giving a fuck, Chip reached into his boxer's and secured his erection behind his belt. With no rap, the tongue wrestling continued. Chip's belt didn't stand a chance; the leather belt popped and his jeans hit the ground.

Cherie ordered, "Get yourself together and let's go."

While attempting to collect his pants, Chip became of balance, and bust his ass. Cherie bust out laughing.

"You shouldn't be laughing girl. That monster won't be popping belts to night, it will be breaking you off," Chip informed her, while shimmying his pants up.

Cherie didn't wait to watch the rest of his shenanigans; instead, she jogged to the driver's side of the vehicle, to get this show on the road. Chip made it to his feet and with one hand holding up his pants, he shuffled to the passenger door. As soon as his butt hit the seat, the gas pedal was mashed to the floor. Chip didn't look back, because he didn't plan on going back.

Ten minutes later, the Bonneville raced at 92 mph on Interstate 80. A green road sign displayed 'Philadelphia 170 Miles'. Since leaving the pen, the lovebirds road in silence. Chip cleared his throat, then broke the ice, "A Baby, it feels like a life sentence since I last saw you."

"Whatever boy, I just saw you last week."

"True, true, true." Chip smiled, then placed his left hand on her thigh. Cherie glanced in his direction, then smiled. "A baby, you should let me drive." Chip licked his lips, then winked.

Cherie popped her lips, then rejected, "You must have been in prison smoking Spice."

"Why are you coming at me like that?"

"Because, you don't have a license and you only want to drive so you can get some sloppy top."

Chip looked out the passenger window, exhaled, then muffled, "What's wrong with a brother trying to get some sloppy top."

"I don't care. You can huff and puff, but I'm not blowing you down. The last time I gave you head behind the wheel, you got cum in my dreads and I went to work looking like the Jamaican version of 'Something about Mary'."

Chip began rolling.

Cherie leered in the goof ball's direction, "Oh, that's funny?"

"Naw, that scene from the movie was stupid."

"Whatever." Cherie sucked her teeth, then continued, "While I'm at it funny man, let's get some rules straight. Rule number one, no anal sex. We didn't do anal before you went to jail and that shit ain't flying now. Rule number two, if you ask for a finger in your butt, it's over."

Are-you-fucking-kidding-me was written all over Chip's face. "Really? Do you think I was on some homo-thug shit in jail?"

"Boy please, I own every season of OZ. And you could have been Adebisi or his main squeeze. Where was I..." She paused to collect her thoughts, then continued issuing her demands, "Rule number three, don't be getting high with my grandma."

"I don't smoke weed and she doesn't even like me."

"That sounds good, but we know weed got the power to spark friendships and orgies. Rule number four..."

Relentlessly, Cherie issued her commandments, until she got a radio signal for Philly's Power 99 FM. She cranked up the volume, as DJ Cosmic Kev screamed, 'Street Banger!' through her car speakers. Cherie was in the zone, reciting Jay-Z's 'I Got the Keys'. Chip formed prayer hands and silently thanked God Cherie's rant was over.

The shadow of night covered Philadelphia, as Cherie exited Route 76, towards Girard Avenue. Chip rolled down the window to take in a whiff of North Philly. Nothing had changed in the hood, from what Chip could see. Chinese Stores and Popi Spots, still owned prime real estate on every other corner. Red bricked row homes, cluttered every block like an endless game of Tetris. Litter, from pampers to shopping carts, landscaped the sidewalks and residents walked around the litter unfazed. Septa buses stopped traffic, providing public transportation for the city. Drug dealers worked every other corner, try to make ends meet. Bums cruised the streets looking on the ground for change or something better. Winos reminisced the good old days, before Cisco Wine was banned in the city and weed came in tan envelopes. Elderly ladies, gossiped about anyone not present at the time. Ockies, in Capri Jeans, hustling oil, incense, and bean pies cruised the avenue promoting goods. And teddy bears placed on the curves, was still a reminder, that North Philly can be a cold place.

Cherie avoided eye contact with Chip as they ventured across Broad Street. 'Wait for it, wait for it,' she thought to herself, bracing for an explosion.

"What the fuck!" Chip detonated, as Cherie turned right on 12th Street. Richard Allen Projects used to look shadier than the first season of 'The Wire'. Trash, piss aroma, graffiti, drug trafficking, and bullets lodged in walls were typical inside the hall ways of Richard Allen's high-rise apartments. On ground zero, violence, drug abuse,

6

and goal-free days caused a vicious cycle for the residents in the public housing row homes.

Back in Chip's day, people were too proud to live in public housing. Now, public housing is beyond Philadelphia's standard of living. Richard Allen's new two-story single-family homes had well-manicured front lawns and fenced off backyards.

"Is my crib gone?" Chip didn't look in Cherie's direction, as the question left his lips.

"Now baby, technically speaking, that jawn was public housing," Cherie corrected him trying to soften the blow.

"This ain't the time to be politically correct." Chip closed his eyes and shook furiously. "Is my house, where I was raised, nurtured, and first cracked on you, at the age of 14, from the second-floor window, gone?"

"That is so sweet, you remember how we met." Chip wasn't amused by her comment and his fingers began to rapidly tap on his thighs. After two right turns, the couple arrived on Warnock Street and she began parallel parking. "My Grandma...."

While the car was still moving, Chip bolted out the passenger door, with one hand securing his pants. On the corner of Warnock & Brown Street, three hustlers reached for their firearms, as Chip dashed in their direction. The corner boys lowered their guard, as Chip turned right on Brown Street.

Seconds later, "Whyyyyyyyyyy!" Chip's howl could be heard 12 blocks out.

Cherie sat on her hood, until Chip emerged on Warnock Street, with his head hung low and feet dragging. One of the hustlers, on the corner of Warnock St, with a high-pitched voice, announced, "Got that tree out old head." Chip waved him off and kept it moving.

Cherie approached Chip and began rubbing his arms. "Are you going to be okay?"

"Hell naw, Richard Allen was a major landmark, like the Staple Center in LA, and I was like Shaq in the paint." Chip began tapping his index finger on Cherie's trunk. "A statue of me, handing off a pack, should be on the corner of 10th & Parrish, for my community service." Chip whacked the trunk this time. "Damn it, Richard Allen projects played a big part in this city's history. Do you know how many people have memories of telling their children, 'don't go to Richard Allen, they'll rob you of everything, plus the baby formula'? Now people will be like, 'Oh, you one of those manicured lawn boujee niggas.'"

Cherie looked away. "It's not that serious."

"The Man," Chip made quotations marks with his fingers, then continued, "has pulled this bullshit and y'all let him. Black people can't keep shit. First Egypt, then Michael Jackson, and now this shit!" Chip hauled ass to the nearest front yard.

"Boy, what are you doing?" Cherie checked her surroundings, hoping no one would witness Chip's folly.

Chip ignored her and proceeded to scissor kick a pink flamingo ornament. Followed by sending a deer ornament into orbit. "Fuck this dollar store, clearance aisle, fugazi shit."

One of the guys on the corner, with a Spanish accent, shouted, "Yo, shut the fuck up."

Before Chip could project his anger down the block, the resident of the vandalized yard, swung open the front door. An older woman, in a blue robe and matching slippers, stood with a pistol grip Mossberg 500, propped on her shoulder. She cocked the shotgun and aimed it in Chip's direction. Chip gave her his undivided attention. The war ready resident spoke in the sweetest church dweller tone, "You know, Jesus hasn't blessed me with everything my heart desired, but I sure do appreciate the little things."

Chip caught her drift and swiftly re-landscaped her lawn, then slowly he retreated with both hands in the air. After his fifth step in reverse, Chip's pants hit the grass.

"Jesus!" The holy woman stumbled backwards. "Deliver me from Sodom and Gomorrah." She tripped and fired a round into her ceiling. "Oh shit, how in the hell am I gonna explain this to public housing?"

Chip scrambled to get himself together, then the couple ran to Cherie's house. While Cherie wrestled with the front door lock, Chip began interrogating, "You let her pull a strap on me. Why didn't you tell her to hand you a box or something?"

"I'm not fighting, no holy rolling old woman, with a gun. Only Destiny Child believe in being a survivor." Cherie rolled her eyes, then made her way in the house. Chip flung his hands in the air but was quick enough to catch his pants this time.

Cherie entered the house unfazed by the aroma in the air. On the other hand, Chip took a mental note, to buy some oils, to counter the smell of curry and chronic in his clothes. Candle lights flickered, as the couple entered a weed and incent clouded living room. Chip spotted pictures of Bob Marley, Emperor Haile Selassie and a large map of Kingston on the living room walls.

Through the thick smoke, Chip spotted Cherie's grandma exhaling a thick cloud of Mary Jane through her nostrils. She tapped the ashes from her spliff into an ashtray, leaned back on the couch, then parked the husky joint in the corner of her mouth. "Rude Boy, the law let you go, huh?" The senior citizen's Caribbean accent was as thick as the day she got off the banana boat.

"Hey Grandma, how…"

Chip was cut off and she cut straight to the chase, "Have ya been keeping your lips to yourself?"

Chip hugged Cherie from behind, then kissed her on the cheek. "It's hard to resist your stunning granddaughter."

"Not Cherie, ya batty boy. I'm talking about the boys on cell block B." She cracked herself up, causing her chubby frame to shake. Chip's right eye began twitching.

"Grandma, be nice," Cherie encouraged her elder.

The elder sucked her teeth. "I should have taken those Ram Squad posters from you. You like those no good, rasclat, shottas," she replied in a tone like she wanted to spit on the ground Chip walked on.

"Nana, you know we don't use that language in this house. Plus, you know your husband use to go to war with the JBM back in the day. He wasn't a saint, but he treated you good, right?" Cherie's grandmother looked away, knowing she couldn't contest the truth.

Cherie took Chip's hand and led him upstairs. The ex-con stumbled on a few stairs, finding it hard to multitask on the stair and Cherie's curves at the same time. She giggled at his lack of concentration, as she led him to her bedroom. After fishing around her wall, she stumbled upon the bedroom light switch. With the flip of the switch, Chip observed his new living quarters. Chip's eye's teared up, comparing his jailhouse cot to her silk covered king size bed. Without warning, Cherie pushed him on the mattress, the door was closed and only the imagination can conceive what happened next.

CHAPTER ONE

On the corner of Warnock and Brown Street, three illegal entrepreneurs observe Cherie and her companion scramble in the house after Ms. Franklin let loose a round.

Shiz's high pitched voice broke the silence. "Who the fuck is bull, hanging with my main squeeze?" The lanky twenty-year-old trembled with rage. Shiz resembled Nipsey Hussle, with three sixty waves and a NP tat on his neck. As usual, he was dressed too loud to be a corner hustler, sporting a Gucci collar shirt, Seven jeans, and Gucci sneakers.

"Shiz, Cherie don't even know your name," Chico, a short 17-year-old Dominican boy with two straight back braids like Jim Jones from Certified Gangster, replied.

Jason, a husky 6'4 brother, decided to add his two cents, "Shiz must be hallucinating off your dust juice, calling Cherie his main

13

jawn; I know he notice her, speed walking in the house, to avoid his creepy eye contact."

Shiz crossed his arms, then spit on the ground. "2 Chinz, I'm not trying to hear that. Real rap, I'm not digging any dude, not from this block, dicking down my jawn. Homeboy gonna make me catch a body."

Chico flagged Shiz off. "Whatever Shiz, you softer than a cookie in milk." Chico turned toward Jason to back him up, but Jason was investigating Cherie's house. "You good Big Homie?"

Jason squinted harder at Cherie's house. "Have you ever seen Cherie bring a dude home?"

Chico shook his head and said, "Naw."

Shiz tapped Jason. "No Meal Left Behind, what are you getting at?"

"Bro, that might be her old man Chip," Jason answered seriously.

Shiz shrugged his shoulders, unimpressed by the name drop. "Never heard of him."

Jason shook his head. "Shiz, how can you rock that NP tat, but don't know the hood legends. That's like saying you're a fan of McDonald, but never heard of a McNugget."

"Why is homeboy on the same level as a McNugget?"

"Chip was famous for making birds move like Alfred Hitchcock."

"I'm glad your man made it into the hood hall of fame, but if he thinks of returning from a death sentence like Jesus, he'll find out how hard it is to move six feet of dirt off a casket." Shiz lifted his Polo shirt, revealing the handle of a forty-five Ruger.

The conversation was cut short, as a middle age man in coveralls approached. "Young bull, let me get two blues and a bag of green." The man leaned back, inspected up and down Brown Street, then passed twenty-five dollars to Shiz.

"Let me get that five," Jason ordered Shiz, while searching his pocket for the pills.

"That's a negative Widebody, you owe me ten dollars."

"Shiz, stop giving my mom IOU's for weed."

"Why? I know your good for it, momma's boy," Shiz reasoned.

"Yo!" the customer erupted. "That weed not gonna smoke itself."

Jason removed a pill bottle, full of Xanies, dumped two blues in his hand, and passed the order to the customer. Shiz removed a sandwich bag, full of 20 sacks of Bubba Kush, removed a dub sack and made the transaction. The pills were quickly ingested, and the weed was tucked in his back pocket.

"Alright gang, be safe out here," the stranger stated with sincerity.

"You too old head," the group responded, and the consumer was on his way. They observed the man until he made a left on 10th Street. Shiz removed a wad of cash and inserted the new profit.

"Praise, be to Allah," Jason said while tapping his pockets.

"Minister Farrakhan, pass off that five you owe me, so you can stay square with the Lord." Shiz extended his hand.

"You got my next sell," answered Jason.

"Cool, I'll let Allah know you're on your financial dean," Shiz Joked.

Chico nodded his head. "It's thurl, how we all have different religions, but we're tighter than brothers. Those goons in the Middle East and Ireland could learn from us. Set trippin in the name of the Lord is super nutty."

"Too Short." Shiz chuckled, then continued, "When it comes to those religious scams, you and Jason are on your own." Shiz rubbed his thumb and index finger together. "In God, we trust."

Chico looked towards the streetlight. "Jesus, help this lunatic."

Shiz looked towards the stars but couldn't find Chico's savior. "A Chico, tell Jesus I got that weed out."

Chico clinched his teeth, while his eyes slowly fell upon Shiz. "Keep being disrespectful and I'm gonna steal you."

"So, your gonna hit me in the name of Jesus?" Shiz shook his head in disgust, then continued, "It's crazy, you were just preaching that holier than thou shit. Look at you now, Hypocrite."

Before Chico and Shiz could go blow for blow, Jason mediated, "Yo, this not Jerry Springer. We on the block."

High beams coming from Brown Street received everyone's undivided attention. A blacked out, stretch Yukon Denali, came to a stop on the corner of Warnock St. The back-passenger window glided down as Shiz approached. Shiz's mother and older boyfriend, Travis, were snuggled up with glasses of Remy Martin's Louis Thirteenth in hand. Shiz sucked his teeth and leered at the couple.

"Hey son," Travis greeted Shiz sounding like Berry Gordy.

"If you're not sending child support my way, you can't call me son. Are we clear Daddy Warbucks?"

"Fall back." Shiz's mother ordered, then got down to business, "We didn't come for all that, we came to tell you that we're taking a trip for the summer."

"Is this the part, where I beg to go with y'all and one of you tell me, maybe next time son," Sarcasm vomited from Shiz's lips.

"Maybe next time son," Travis said with a smile.

17

"No trip, no check, who are you fooling? I should steal you for lying to my face."

"Boy, I would tell you off, but we don't have time for that. Travis and I are heading to Martha's Vineyard and you need to handle your business. Now recite momma's rules." She demanded, then took a sip of the fifty dollars a shot cognac.

Shiz slowly exhaled, then commenced, "Don't spend all the EBT cash at the beginning of the month. Don't buy blunts using the EBT card. Never be late paying public housing for our rent. No stashing drugs in the house. No ifs ands or maybes, when it comes to having babies. No, my girl cannot move in. No smoking your weed. No drinking your Taylors Port. And make up my bed first thing in the morning."

"That's my baby," she sounded prouder than a mother at a spelling bee. "Now toss me two sacks, it's gonna be a long trip."

"What do I look like, handing you free weed, when you're rolling with Daddy Warbucks."

She snapped her head in Travis direction. "You heard the man."

"Son, let me get three for fifty."

"You rich and still cutting deals in the hood. That's how the rich stay rich and the poor stay poor." Shiz shook his head, then countered, "Stop calling me son and you can get six for a hundred."

After making the quick exchange, his mother stepped out the limo, donning an elegant evening dress. She was in her upper-thirties, but black don't crack and she could pass for twenty something. The two exchanged a firm hug and Shiz kissed her on the cheek. She gazed deep into Shiz's eyes. "I love you baby."

"Love you too momma," Shiz returned.

"I love you too son," Chico joked.

"Chico, shut your joe ass up," Shiz barked.

"Hi Chico. Hi Jason," greeted Ms. Smith.

"Hi Ms. Smith," The two sung in harmony.

Shiz's mother returned to the vehicle and stuck her head out the window. "Don't forget my rules, be safe out here and I'll see you soon."

"Alright son, you know the rules," Travis put in his two cents.

"Travis, shut your Joe ass up, before I cancel your Bengay rub down." Ms. Smith sounded like the female version of Shiz.

Shiz looked like he wanted to throw up. "Ain't nobody trying to hear that."

"Forgive me baby." Travis snapped his finger, then pointed forward.

The Yukon slowly pulled from the curve and Shiz rejoined his crew. Jason patted Shiz on the back. "Don't worry about Travis. He's just like all my momma's boyfriends. Here today and gone tomorrow."

"Unlike you Jason, I'm not whacking my momma's boyfriend to have him gone tomorrow."

"I'm Innocent until proven guilty, my brother."

"True," Chico mimicked 2 Chainz once again.

Silence fell upon the Warnock Crew, as Major marched in their direction. His uniform of the day was camouflage pants, tightly laced steel toe black boots, and a t-shirt that read, 'Don't blame it on the PTSD'. Major approached the regiment with a salute. Jason and Chico chuckled at Shiz as he returned the salute.

"At ease grunts," Major directed the crew, then eyeballed Chico, "Shorty due whop, I need…" Abruptly, Major's eyes expanded to full capacity. "Hit the deck," Major shouted, then belly flopped on the ground. The fearful hustlers followed suit, putting their dick in the dirt and hands over their head.

Chico was the first to check if the coast was clear, then he snapped on his dysfunctional customer, "Major, you shot the fuck out. Have you been going to your VA appointments?"

Warnock crew beat the dirt off their clothing as they ascended to their feet. The wounded warrior leaped to his feet, stood at attention, then parade rest. "That bitch at the hospital don't know me. She says I got post-traumatic stress from the war. I asked that bitch what war?" Major presented his hand and began counting. "I'm from Richard Allen, I served in the Gulf War, I survived the crack era and I got five baby mommas. Now, them bitches should be classified as weapons of mass destruction."

"Frontline, I'm not serving you tonight. You drawlin already and you're not even wetted," Chico informed his unstable customer.

"Immigrant, I'm good." Major's right eye twitched as he presented a fake smile.

"Save the lies for the disability board. We not having another episode of you clearing houses with an imaginary shotgun."

"Really Pablo? That was training."

"Who the fuck is Pablo?" Chico questioned, then continued, "See, statements like that, is why you're not getting wetted tonight. The best we can do for you is weed or blues."

"I got bottles of Ritalin, if I wanted to space out all damn night. Skipper, let me get a dipper."

Chico folded his arms. "Major, you're not getting served tonight."

"Those Ricans down Badlands, will serve me, plus give me a military discount. How are you helping the troops?" Major preformed an about face and marched off into the night. Once the Vet hit 10th Street, he made a left face turn and began jogging toward Girard Ave. The crew bust out laughing.

"Major is shot the fuck out," stated Shiz.

"Do you think he gonna jog his dysfunctional ass to Badlands tonight?" Chico asked his crew.

"I remember seeing Major jogging around Front & Olney, during a heat wave, rocking tight sweatpants and a white beater," Jason replied.

"That's miles from here," Chico perceived.

"A Jason, maybe Major can train you, so you can get that chin off your chin," Shiz clowned.

"You always trying to play somebody, with your whomp whomp jokes," Jason responded.

Before Shiz could compound insults on Jason, red and blue lights reflecting off nearby homes, instantly killed the tranquil vibe. They turned to the sight of a white Charger flying in their direction. The boys froze, as the Charger screeched to a halt.

A chubby black officer eventually squeezed out the passenger side of the vehicle. "Freeze, you WIC cereal babies," the officer instructed while struggling to remove his firearm.

Jason spoke up, with his arms folded, "What's the problem officer?"

Shiz spoke up before the officer could reply, "Besides a gut too big to view your gun or dick."

Officer Kemp's nostrils flared like a raging bull, as he ascended the curve. Teddy bears and candles, that were displayed on the sidewalk, were booted out of the pissed officer's way.

From a window across the street, a young man's voice screamed out, "Yo, that's my brother's memorial."

The chubby white officer, in the driver seat, stuck his head out the window. "Well, come pick it up, you littering bastard."

"Ok, you want to be disrespectful?" The rage from the window was lethal.

"Kemp hurry up," the white officer ordered. "We could be patting down hookers around Hunting Park."

"Ew!" Shiz looked discussed. "Most of them jawns are transsexuals. How high do y'all frisk on those suspects?"

Furiously, the officer rushed towards Shiz. Shiz closed his eyes, bracing for police brutality. Before officer Kemp could get within arm's reach, shots ringed out from an automatic weapon. The distressed officer spun around, took two steps and dove to grab a hold of the passenger window. As the Charger sped away, Officer Kemp held on for dear life.

Once the shooter ceased fire, Warnock Crew put the memorial back in order, then gave a salute to their hero.

"Let's bounce, before the whole 18th District slide through," Jason recommended. With no rap, they took off towards their homes.

CHAPTER TWO

10:35 p.m. was the time Chip read on the bathroom's wall clock. After verifying the time, he looked over his appearance in the mirror. Chip sported a red Polo button up, blue Guess jeans, and Timberland boots purchased two days before being incarcerated. He also sported enough jewelry to outshine most rappers on the front cover of the Source Magazine. He removed some Amber White oil from his pocket and applied it. Chip pulled down his Phillies cap to his eyebrow, turned off the light, then made his way down stairs.

Chip usually passed Cherie's grandma without her glancing in his direction. Today, Ms. Marley took a triple take. "Cherie, the jailbird looks like he's ready to fly the coup," announced the seasoned comedian.

Chip paid her no mind, as he made his way to the kitchen. Cherie was sitting at the kitchen table, sporting pajama pants, slippers and a throwback, 'Do the Right Thing' t-shirt. She was biting her bottom lip, stimulated by the words in Zane's classic, 'Sex Chronicles' novel. The book had her undivided attention, to the point she didn't notice Chip enter the room. Chip snuck up and kissed her on the neck.

"Oh, yes daddy," Cherie moaned loudly, then slammed a hand over her mouth. After regaining her composure, she looked Chip up and down with approval. "You want to play dress up and take off tonight? I'll undress you with my teeth." She chopped her teeth in Chip's direction.

Chip looked at the ceiling and shook his head. He folded his arms, then returned his gaze to her. "Naw Cherie, I'm about to bounce."

After slowly putting down the novel, untwisting her lips, she spoke up, "Where do you think you're going? I'm not dressed." She cocked her head to the right.

"I'm about to hit Onyx."

"You think you going to blow our money on some fake butt bitches? Boy, you must be smoking with my grandma."

"Re, I only got eight stacks on me."

"I don't care if you only had the admission fee, you not blowing our money on those fuck for a buck bitches." Like a bipolar chick, her attitude quickly changed. "How about, you make it rain on me and I'll guarantee you a happy ending."

25

"Re, I got to get out of this house. My days consist of Netflix, Martin reruns and knocking you off."

She gave him the Peoples Eye Brow. "Oh, I'm boring?"

"Naw baby, that thing be snapping, but I need to get out."

"Alright, roll out…"

Chip cut her off, "Cool." Pecked her on the cheek and prepared to exit.

Cherie shot to her feet. "Boy, get your black ass over here, and give me that jewelry and cash. We got plans and you acting like Johnny Law don't keep tabs on ex-king pens."

"You and the man robbing me of my freedom," Chip complained but did as told. After flashing him a fake smile, she returned to her seat and began reading again. Chip looked puzzled as he ventured to the front door. "What am I gonna do now?"

After exiting the house, Chip contemplated his next move. After realizing, a man without money can only open limited doors, Chip felt stuck. While pacing back and forth, a woman walking to the corner caught his attention. The woman stopped at the corner and made a transaction with the three boys. The fact that they didn't walk off to a drug stash baffled Chip. After 10 minutes of observing their enterprise, he noted infinite flaws in their operation. Chip's conscious was eating him, to go school those suckers in the art of drug dealing. His conscious won and he was off to the corner.

Chico sales pitched Chip as he approached, "Got that workout my man."

"Do y'all always promote to strangers?" asked Chip.

Jason stepped to Chip. "Who do you think you are, the better business bureau?"

"You must be looking to get promoted to head chef in prison; serving every Tom, Dick, and Harry with little prejudgment," Chip said confidently, unshaken by the mass of Jason.

Shiz also stepped to Chip. "You must have lost your mind, coming to Warnock Street, telling us, we're running a shitty operation?"

"I haven't lost my mind." Chip paused and smiled. "I used to be the plug or extorter of all drug dealers in and around Richard Allen. My name is Chip."

Jason nodded his head up and down like a bobblehead, while taking three steps back. Shiz followed Jason's moves and backed off Chip.

"I'll take it that y'all heard of me. So, what's your names?"

Shiz looked Chip up and down. "Dawg, we not sweet. Don't think you going to extort us."

"Why would I extort y'all?" Chip smirked. "I would just murder y'all and train a hungry crew that's teachable." Chip paused and nodded his head in agreement with his plan. "That sounds more profitable to me." The crew had no comment and Chip repeated his question. "So, what's your names?"

"I'm Jason, the skinny bull is Shiz, and my Dominican homie is Chico."

"Chip, what's your angle?" inquired Chico.

"I want to help your team increase profits and decrease risk." Chip checked his surroundings, then continued, "Yaw Strapped?"

Shiz flashed his forty-five. Chip looked at Jason with the stink face, as he removed a twenty-two revolver from his underwear. Chico jogged off and returned with a duffle bag. Chip's eyelids blew back, as Chico removed an AK forty-seven with a banana clip.

Chip spazzed out, "Get that chopper away from me. Don't you know, it's five years for the gun and a year for every bullet in the clip in Philly?"

"You asked if we were strapped. And as my cousin Rell would say, 'I would rather be judged by twelve, then carried by six'," Chico theorized, as he placed the assault rifle back into the duffle bag.

Chico jogged off to return his hardware and Jason placed his twenty-two back in to is underwear. As soon as Chico returned, Chip began his speech. "If I were y'all, I'd…"

Shiz waved his hands back and forth, "Save your spill for a losing team. We winners like any team with Shaq in the paint. You like Karl Malone trying to tell Jordan how to get a ring."

"Your team, is one investigation away from telling y'all story to some Scared Straight kids," Chip informed Shiz.

"Chip, don't worry about Shiz, bless us with your knowledge," Jason pleaded.

"Bless us with your knowledge," Shiz mocked his friend in a woman's voice. "You sound like a Lil Wayne groupie."

"Well gang, I guess y'all good for now. I'll be around, if all y'all change your minds," Chip emphasized on the word 'all y'all', as he eye balled Shiz.

"Chip forget about him, we are down." Chico pointed at Jason and himself.

"It's a waste of time. Everyone must play their part or my master plan will never work. Plus, outsiders are known to snitch, if shit hits the fan."

"Don't worry about our plan. You should be focusing on filling out those applications and keeping your piss clean for the man," stated Shiz.

Chip nodded his head. "Like I said before, I'll be around. And remember this, 'A hustler with no instruction, is bound for self-destruction," Chip dropped that jewel, then stepped off.

Jason questioned the know it all, "Shiz, why are you drawlin?"

"Big Mac, why you dick eating?" Shiz returned.

"Shiz, we could have at least heard him out," responded Chico.

"If you're looking for a savior read the bible. We straight out here, yi mean?" Shiz paused, as he saw someone heading their way. "Fuck that small talk, we got paper heading this way," said Shiz and the crew returned to their normal operation.

CHAPTER THREE

On a beautiful Saturday afternoon, Cumberland Street was swarming with folks looking to purchase pot. A patrol car, on the payroll, monitored the drug trafficking with zero interest in interfering. Not only did the cops profit off the drug trade, so did the Chinese Store and Beer Distributor; who earn millions off tobacco products and munchies.

Jason observed Cumberland Street's economy from the rear-view mirror of his silver 2004 Marauder. Jason spotted Shiz traveling at a swift pace exiting the Chinese Store.

As soon as Shiz open the passenger door, Jason cut into him, "Were you discussing the quality of weed in the city or starting a weed man union?"

"Naw, Jenny Craigless, it was a traffic jam. You know old ladies don't grab bud after dark."

"I don't get it, why do y'all potheads go out y'all way to cop bud from Cumberland. If it's not you asking for a ride up here, it's my momma," Jason said with disgust.

"First and foremost, never get high on your own supply. You should know that, Biggie Not Small. Secondly, my weed cost a dub a pop and Cumberland sell nicks of funk. Yi Mean?" Shiz extended his hand for a handshake.

"I don't smoke," Jason responded soberly and left Shiz's hand in the wind.

"You suppose to agree with me no matter what," Shiz informed Jason

"No, I'm your man, because I keep it one hundred with you, no matter what."

"Well, to keep it a bean with you, I need you to make another stop."

Are you kidding me, was written all over Jason's face. "When did I become Morgan Freeman from driving Ms. Daisy? We need to head back to the block. Chico grinding by himself and it's a block party going down."

"Drive me to Cambria and Stillman, I'll give you five dollars."

"What are you grabbing from killer Cambria?"

"Homeboy, who just served me, said they got baggies at the Chinese Store on Stillman."

Jason presented his hand. "Pay up."

"Really, you think I'm gonna burn you?" Shiz asked in disbelief.

"Shiz, I'm doing this for my own protection. You are known for putting a blunt in the air and telling everybody they're trying to burn you because 'you're high'."

Shiz looked out the window to hide his smirk, then he turned to Jason with a goofy look on his face. "You know that bud makes me paranoid baby."

A nice size bankroll was removed from Shiz's pocket and a five-dollar bill was sent Jason's way. Jason held the bill up to the sunlight, then shoved it in his pocket.

After checking traffic, Jason pulled from the curve. A red stop light halted Jason's progress and Shiz decided to sales pitch a random guy at the bus stop. "A my man, do you blow tree?" Shiz asked while imitating someone smoking a cigar.

The stranger began approaching the car. "What'chu got?"

Before Shiz could respond, Jason mashed the gas and made a right on York Street. "Is this International Test Your Friendship Day? I would have fucked you up, if he was an undercover cop or stick up kid," Jason bowed his head and took his hand off the wheel to repent. "Allah, keep me on my dean, in this world of folly."

Shiz quickly grabbed the wheel and pleaded with Jason, "Yo, grab the wheel! You and the Most High, need to connect at the Mosque, not while driving." Jason complied and Shiz would have continued to get in Jason's ass, but the song 'Home of Philly' caught his attention. He turned up the volume and began reciting the hook.

> The home of Philly
> Where the fiends on every corner
> Dope heads on every other
> The jails got all the fathers
> The coke got all the mothers y'all
> Baby on one

MICHAEL HIGGINS JR.

Dope up in the other arm

Another crack baby born

They've got us trapped crazy y'all

The home of Philly where they cook out everyday

Raid the block every other

The hustlers on every corner

The cops on every other y'all

Niggas will "shoot"

And think nothing of it ch'all

Bodies every other y'all

But we gotta love it ch'all

The home of Philly

As the car made a left turn on 22nd and Cambria, Jason turned down the radio and shook his head at the sight of teddy bears and a child's portrait in front of an elementary school. "They don't even care about the babies around here." Jason planted his right hand over his heart.

"Stop bitching dawg, I got you," Shiz said, then checked the lock on his door.

Cambria Street looked sketchier than O.J. speeding in the Bronco. The alleys were littered with everything from diapers to washing machines. Goons patrolled the hood with hands in their pockets and heads on a swivel. Junkies carried everything from radios to satellite dishes, to the pawn shops on 22nd Street.

A patrol vehicle, stopped at a red light, on 24th Street. As Jason came to a stop next to the patrol vehicle, the cop looked up tight. Jason presented a smile to the officer, attempting to calm the officer's nerves. The patrol vehicle peeled rubber, nearly clipping the tail end of a trash truck.

Jason's head snapped in Shiz's direction, "No funny stuff out here. Get in and get out. OK?"

"Damn Jason, I wanted four wings and fries."

"Whatever bro, just stick to the script," said Jason, as the light turned green.

Shiz pointed to an open parking spot. "Pullover, we're here."

Jason paralleled parked in front of the Chinese Store. Cautiously, Shiz exited the car and looked over both shoulders twice. Mountains of pictures, teddy bears, and candles were planted in front of a boarded-up house across the street.

"Got that green out," a voice screamed out, causing Shiz to pop to attention. With a quick glance, Shiz noticed five goons posted with all eyes on him, on the corner of Bambrey Street.

Shiz looked for comfort in the direction of his partner. Hope was demolished, as Shiz heard the passenger door lock. Shiz barked, "Yo, come on," while rapidly knocking on the passenger window.

Jason rolled down the passenger window and looked at Shiz like he was stupid. "What do you mean, 'come on'?"

"Fam, this ain't the time to be shook daddy. Come on!" Shiz repeated.

Jason examined the memorial across the street, then retorted, "Shiz, it looks like the Vietnam Memorial across the street and I wasn't drafted."

"Jason, man up," Shiz sounded like a football coach. "The store is only 12 feet away and you Big Jason."

"What is 12 divided by two?" Shiz began subtracting fingers. Jason decided to continue, "Six feet deep."

"Jason, get your husky ass out the car or I'm telling Chico. You know I'm gonna bring this shit up for at least two weeks."

Jason exhaled while reaching for the car door handle. Shiz waited until Jason reached the curve to move forward. The exterior of the Chinese Store was a bulletproof glass. Bullets were lodged in the glass, which confirmed the glass did work. Oddly, only one name was spray painted on the glass, which read, 'REESE'. Inside of the store, the counter was made of bulletproof plexiglass. A person with dreadlocks was leaning on the wall, with a hat pulled down low enough to conceal their identity. An elderly man, with bags in his hands, made his way to the exit.

While ascending the two steps of the Chinese Store, Shiz decided to sell pitch the gentleman, "Got that tree out."

The elder viciously shook his head no.

Jason barked at Shiz, "Are you crazy? This is not the hood to be selling to random people."

Shiz ignored Jason's words of wisdom and proceeded to enter the Chinese Store. As soon as Jason crossed the thresh hole, the right arm of the mystery person swung from behind the back and a chrome long nose forty-four revolver was waved in the intruder's direction. The nonverbal communication was comprehended and the Warnock two raised their hands.

"Who gave y'all the Ok, to serve out here," the mystery character interrogated. The head raised on the unidentified gunslinger and confusion took hold of the two defendants. The long nose revolver petrified, while the lips and eyes on the gunslinger screamed, 'bad chick alert'.

Shiz spoke up first, "Before you go any further, I got to say, you are making that Aaliyah look work." Shiz snapped his finger.

"Do you not see this gun pointed in your direction?" she asked, then proceeded to speak slowly as if they were Special Ed students, "What the fuck are y'all thinking, trying to move tree on my block?"

"Sweetheart, he..."

Jason was quickly cut off, "Nigga, you don't know me like that, calling me pet names. Y'all keep fucking around and Teddy Pendergrass will be giving y'all game."

Both men swallowed hard in fear. The armed woman's attention shifted to something outside the Chinese Store. She looked back at the boys and in a slow skin-crawling tone she ordered, "Don't fucking move." The boys closed their eyes anticipating the first shot. Their eyes jolted open, when they heard a friendly feminize voice scream, "Keya!" The gunwoman, gestured someone to come in the store with her free hand.

An Asian woman emerged from behind a two-door display cooler. "Reese, you tell Keya to come here?"

"Le, why you saying my name?" the armed women nodded at her gun.

The Asian woman folded her arms. "You just say Keya name and you just said my name."

"Bitch, it's a difference," Reese said while pointing at the firearm.

"Le, it is a difference," Jason confirmed.

"Shut the fuck up, before I find out if your fat ass bleed Yoo-hoo!" Reese responded through clenched teeth. Jason zipped his lips and threw away the key.

Shiz cracked up. "She said Yoo-hoo!"

Jason looked at Shiz like he was crazy. Then everyone's attention went towards the Chinese Store entrance, as a young girl wearing a white scarf around her head, white t-shirt, looney tunes pajama pants, and dusty Tweety Bird slippers entered. Keya was rapidly patting the side of her head. "Wait 'til I leave to shoot these bulls, that gun is too loud."

"Shoot in the head. No big mess," Le added her two cents.

"Le, you actin like your lazy ass is going to clean up their corpse. You know I don't leave evidence," Reese responded.

"What do you want Reese?" Keya sounded five minutes passed annoyed.

Reese popped her lips. "Tell your mom, I saw this bag that I want her to grab for me, at King of Prussia Mall."

"Keya, come, come. I need your mom to boost for me too," Le said while waving in Keya's direction.

"Le, call me like a dog again and I will be shoplifting in North Hills. Yi mean?"

Le looked nervous and confused. "How do you know where I live?"

"Don't worry about that bitch, what the fuck do you want?" Keya strolled in front of Reese's revolver, headed to the counter.

"Hold on, I got pictures of the skirt on my phone." Le disappeared.

"Hurry up or I may reconsider boosting at your crib." Keya giggled while turning around. She leaned on the plexiglass and leered at the two strangers. "What up with these bitch ass niggas?"

Reese shrugged her shoulders. "They think they can sell tree out here."

Keya pointed towards the mountain of Hallmark's finest mementos outside. "Are y'all blind or stupid?"

Jason pointed towards Shiz. "Reese, he was in LD classes…"

Jason was quickly cut off. "Who said you can use my name? I didn't accept your friend request on Facebook."

"We here, because I heard this store sold baggies," Shiz spit out as fast as humanly possible.

A smile came upon Reese's face, "What size you need?"

"You sell baggies?" questioned Shiz.

Reese moved to the left, revealing a baggy display on the wall. "Did you think Le ran shit around here? She is on the payroll, moving my work. I even got cops on staff around here. If Johnny Law caught me putting one in you, they would ask, 'If I want your body to hit the news or their trunk?" Reese paused to conceal her firearm. "What size baggies do you need?"

By the time the two boys left the Chinese Store, Reese and Shiz were communicating like old friends catching up. Jason was puzzled, how two people could hold a twenty-minute conversation, on how the size of bags can affect the attitude of their customers.

"I'll holla at you Reese." Shiz farewelled Reese, before flopping down on the passenger seat.

Reese waved back, "Be safe and get to church. Jesus is the light and salvation."

"Jason Shabazz, did you hear that?" Shiz asked, being a smart ass.

"Why do you think Muslims don't bang with Jesus?" Jason shook his head, "Why do I even bang with you?" Jason asked himself, as he started the car.

"You hang with me because I'm the bull that just got us out of that crazy situation." Shiz tapped his chest proudly.

"We wouldn't have gotten into that situation if you were smart enough to understand that Philly is not a free drug trade zone." Before Jason could pull off, he noticed a car rolling backward down Cambria Street. The driver and passenger were sleep, with no sign of waking soon. Jason tapped Shiz to check out the action, "Shiz, look at those fools."

"It's too early to be pancaked. They need Jesus, what do you think Mr. Shabazz?" Shiz paused, then continued, "Do you think they need some green, to go with their syrup and pills?" Shiz grabbed the handle of the door. "I should check."

"You must want to get left around here," Jason said, without a joking bone in his body.

"Saying what you just said, how you just said it, I think it's time to rout." Shiz fastened his seat belt.

The car pulled from the curve. Jason and Shiz, looked down Bambrey Street as they passed. The block was full of action, like the New York Stock Exchange. Buyers were yelling "Yurp" and "Yo"; and sellers got right to the point, asking, "How many". Jason reclined in his seat, as he came to a stop sign on 26th Street. But the sight of a young man sprinting across 27th Street made Jason lean up. Seconds later, gunfire erupted. The fearful driver mashed the gas, while simultaneously making a left turn. Jason flew through countless stop signs, with no sign of slowing down.

Shiz had had enough, after his head slammed against the passenger window, during a left turn onto Dauphin Street. "Ricky Bobby, slow this mother fucker down, you got me seeing double."

"My bad bro, but you know bullets don't have no names." Jason quoted the little girl from 'Boys in the Hood'.

Jason slammed on the brakes, as a drug dealer boldly walked in the middle of the street to make a sale. The dealer ice grilled Jason, while slowly returning to the sidewalk.

"Did you see that?" Jason shook his head at America's worst nightmare.

"The DVD Man need to sell him a season of The Wire," Shiz stated and Jason agreed via head nod.

As Jason crossed Broad Street, a smile came upon his face. "It's crazy on that side of Broad Street. We got class on the Eastside of Broad."

"Class." Shiz chuckled, then continued, "Check out your classy citizens." Shiz pointed toward four brothers wearing ski masks, carrying an ATM out of a corner store. "They should just call Fox News now, so they can put in their bid for the top story." Jason laughed at Shiz's sarcasm. "If they call Action

News right now, they could get a jump on the reward money." Shiz cleared his throat, then continued, "Speaking of money, your mom grabbed two dubs this morning, on your credit."

Jason punched the steering wheel, "She supposed to be budgeting."

"What you gonna do, momma's boy." Shiz sported a Kool-Aid smile.

"I'm not a momma's boy, she needs me in her corner, because these men ain't shit now in days."

"You sound as dysfunctional as a Tyler Perry character."

"Is it crazy, to care for your mother?"

"Why can't her boyfriend take care of her? O yea, you're a momma's boy."

"Those guys don't want to stick around during the hard times."

"It's hard to stick around, once you become a missing person report," Shiz countered.

"What do those guys going missing have to do with me?" Jason asked innocently.

"Jason, I helped you carry that last husky bull to your trunk."

"We can't have the law investigating our operation because some fool slipped down the stairs."

"You right, anyone could slip from the top of some plush carpeted stairs." Jason couldn't help but laugh at Shiz's quick wit.

"On a serious note." Jason looked at Shiz. "Don't tell Chico about our run in with Reese. You know I'm his role model."

"The blind leading the blind," said Shiz.

"You must be deaf because you don't hear anything when the wise are talking."

"I don't hear them because I'm counting money, fucking bitches, at the same damn time," Shiz bounced in his seat, as he recited the rap lyrics.

"You sure? I thought it had to do with you being in those Special Ed classes. Don't think I forgot about your slow days at William Penn." Jason teased.

"Whatever, I was smart enough to sell candy to every student in those classes, plus the teachers."

Jason slapped his belly. "Supporting that business is probably why I'm so husky today."

"Naw, you husky from eating those seconds, thirds, and leftovers," Shiz cracked.

"You're so insensitive."

"Fuck out of here, you just called me retarded."

"Shiz, I have been fighting this battle for years." Jason got emotional.

"You sound like Oprah from The Color Purple, 'All my life I had to fight'," Shiz mimicked the billionaire perfectly, then continued, "Plus, you got a fast food black card. How does that help the situation?"

"I earned that card because I have A1 credit. If you did the same, you wouldn't be treating me like a Hackman."

"If I did the same, we would look like Biggie and Heavy D in a Pinto." Shiz puffed up his cheeks.

"I would be Heavy D, you got that cockeyed thing going on."

"Fuck what you talking about, I'm ready to get my Biggie on at the block party. I know your mom is going ham on that grill, without the swine." Shiz began to daydream.

"I would be on my fourth plate if I wasn't' you're underpaid Uber man."

MICHAEL HIGGINS JR.

"Well Uber man, step on it!"

CHAPTER FOUR

Parking was tight throughout Richard Allen, but Jason found a park without having to spin the block. Jason examined the space between two parked cars, then turned to Shiz. "Do you think I can fit?"

Shiz looked Jason up and down, "In the car or out?"

"You want to eat or not?"

"Has anyone ever asked you that question?"

"Stop playing or you'll find out what would of happen to that little white girl, if she stuck around in a bear's house."

Shiz examined the parking space, "Your whip game weak, but you can fit." Shiz looked around and noticed a man posted by the car behind them. The passenger window rolled down and Shiz head popped out.

Jason manhandled Shiz back onto his seat. "Didn't we just talk about you promoting to strangers out of my car?"

"Damn Mighty Joe Young, I was just going to ask bull to make sure we don't hit the car behind us."

Jason released his grip and Shiz popped his head back out the window. "Yurp!" Shiz caught the gentlemen's attention, "Can you make sure we don't hit the car behind us?"

"Young bull, I got you. Don't worry about a thing," the stranger sounded happier than a smoker being offered a tester.

Shiz turned to Jason. "I hope old head don't think we're tipping him."

"Shiz, not everybody in Philly is on the come up. Now be quiet, so I can concentrate." Jason turned to the stranger, "I'm coming back, look out for me."

"I got you scrap." The stranger took a knee and put a hawk eye on the situation. Jason put his car in reverse and slowly traveled backward. "Come on baby, punch it in reverse and you got it."

Jason pulled forward out of the park, believing he was too close for comfort. The stranger became hysterical, "Are you shitting me? I know you listened to that square at the DMV, now pay attention. When I say hit it, you hit it."

Jason had heard enough, "I got this old head, go handle your business."

"Young bull, let me be your Phil Jackson and make me." He cleared his throat, then continued, "I mean you, a winner."

"I'm cool ock, go handle your business." Jason raised up in his seat and punched it hard in reverse.

"Here we go," the man said to himself, as he straddled the curve like a baseball catcher over the mound. Jason whipped the car to the right, then simultaneously slammed on the brake while whipping the car to the left. The car was perfectly parallel to the curve, but the vehicle still traveled at a snail's pace in reverse. Jason pulled the emergency brake, but it wasn't enough to stop his car from tapping the car behind him. The car alarm howled.

Instantaneously, the stranger sprung to his feet. "I'm hit, man down!" The con-artist slapped his forehead and flopped to the ground. "Where is that gecko, in these times of injustice?"

As Jason pulled forward, Shiz spoke up, "I guess you're right again, everyone in Philly is not scheming."

"I got this clown, watch this."

Both boys exited the car at the same time. Jason walked around to the curve, observed the back of his car, then glanced at the con artist with grandeur in his eyes. Jason shook his head and walked in the opposite direction. "You wasted your time, I don't have insurance."

"Got em!" Shiz yelled, while pointing at the unlucky conman.

The swindler scrambled to his feet and screamed out, "Look out for me young bull and move your car; I'm trying to get a check. Ni mean?"

"Fuck out of here ock. Go YouTube a new hustle," Shiz responded and kept it moving.

Caution tape and plastic lawn chairs secured the block party at each end of Warnock Street. Cooks barbecued on grills of all sizes. Smiling faces were in abundance in every direction. The DJ shouted into the microphone, "All the ladies that still got money from the first of the month, scream AHHHHHH!" Some women screamed loud, other just waved their EBT card in the air. Single men and baby mommas were doing the two step to LL's 'Who Do You Love'. Unhappily, Sons watched their mother's dance with hopefully not another sperm donor. Fast young girls were twerking offbeat to LL's classic. Another group of girls watched two friends slap box over who would be holding the rope next for Double Dutch. Hungry neighbors were curing the munchies, with paper plates piled high with everything from watermelon to steak. Older women constantly patted sweat off their heads but continued to drink from red cups full of Taylor Port or Manischewitz. A couple young adults were praying for deuces, playing Pity Pat for a dollar a hand.

Chico was spotted, leaning on the street light pole, on the corner of Brown Street. Jason and Shiz approached Chico with handshakes.

"What's the deal cannon?" Jason asked Chico.

"We looking like money big homie," Chico was hype, then he looked at Jason and Shiz suspiciously, "What took y'all so long?"

Jason looked at Shiz with the 'don't say shit face', then turned to Chico and chuckled before proceeding, "It's block parties on every other block today. Yi mean?"

Chico nodded his head in agreement, then reached into each of his back pockets, and passed off his crew's profit from today. Chico looked at the ground before making his next statement, "Oh yea, Chip said, we should close up shop for today."

Shiz flung his arms in the air. "I know you're not going to let that handicapped hustler slow us down. Selling drugs during a block party, is easier money than passing a collection plate around people looking for hope. We about to come up like the first of the month. Y'all down right?" Shiz's charisma was in overdrive.

"I'm down. Momma wants to see a play in New York and you know I..." Jason thought about it and flipped out, "New York! Ain't no New York popping off around here. She got some explaining to do." Jason pushed his crew out the way to confront his mom.

Chico turned to Shiz, "What is he talking about?"

"2 Chinz told me, he put his momma on a weed allowance."

Chico chuckled, "He shot out for that. She needs a hobby or a hustle. All she does is smoke weed, clean, watch Own, and cook for Jason." Chico and Shiz turned to watch the drama unfold.

Shiz nodded his head as he checked out Jason's mom. Ms. Shabazz wore a white superwomen t-shirt, light blue jean, and Air Max Nikes, looking like the hood version of Kelly Rowland. "Jason's mom bad as shit. He lucky I'm not South Philly slimy." Shiz turned to Chico, "You know she asked me to smoke with her, while Jason was at the Mosque. And you know." Shiz performed quotation fingers, while finishing his statement, "'let's smoke', Is code for, 'let's fuck'."

"I'm hip. This jawn from Logan wants me to come smoke with her, but you know I can't lie to Abuela. My grandma is the Dominican version of Judge Judy."

Jason was too far away for his crew to ease drop, but it looked like he was giving his mom an ear full. People close by, stopped what they were doing, to be nosy. Jason's verbal assault came to a ceasefire, as soon as his mom began whimpering into her palms. Someone in the crowd cried out, "Poor pothead!"

Jason took his mother in his arms. After a few comforting words, Jason returned to the corner and got right down to business. "Lend me a dub sack, my mom said I blew her high."

Shiz let out a slight chuckle. "You told her."

"Shiz, I was drawlin coming at her sideways, like she smoking meth or something. Obama smoked weed and look where he landed."

"Whatever Dr. Phil. One dub sack, coming right up." Shiz began rumbling through his pockets.

"Chico, you feel me, right?" Jason inquired.

"Mi no speaka any English."

Before Jason could respond to Chico's smart-ass comment, Shiz placed the order in Jason's palm. "I owe you," Jason told Shiz, then returned to his mom. Ms. Shabazz gave him a kiss on the cheek, then sent him on his way. Jollily Jason skipped away and clicked his heels.

Chico and Shiz were so caught up in Jason's foolishness, that they didn't notice the black Tahoe creep up behind them. "Break yourself fool," the driver screamed out. Chico nor Shiz flinched, they instantly recognized Turk's suburban Turkish accent.

"Turk, what did I tell you about creeping up on black people? You lucky I didn't pull out something big enough to flip your Tahoe," Shiz yelled in Turk's direction.

"Shiz, you're not a shooter." Turk flagged off his client.

"Whatever, park that gas guzzler and holla at me." With no rap, Turk sped from the curve.

The model momma's boy cheesed, as he strolled back to the corner. That smile evaporated, as he was shoved out the way by Chico's grandma's cane. Ms. Perez hobbled pass Jason's eclipsing frame, with all the speed a seventy-six-year-old could muster. Chico's eyes scrambled in fear, knowing something was horribly wrong; if she was off the couch for anything other than the bathroom, kitchen, market, or church service. Chico forged a quivering smile.

"Jesus!" Ms. Perez bellowed Chico's legal name.

"Hey Abuela, why aren't you watching Telemundo?" Chico rambled. In mid-stride, Ms. Perez crashed her cane against Chico's left knee. Chico collapsed to the pavement, bracing his wound. "Como?" he questioned in agony.

Jason and Shiz approached Ms. Perez with open arms and they both received a kiss on the forehead. Ms. Perez returned her focus on her injured grandson. "On the ground like a puta." She shook her head and her turkey neck followed suit. Chico hesitantly made it to his feet. "Are you too important to see if I'm hungry. That el pollo smells muy bien. You think

58

black people are the only people that like Chicken? If it wasn't for beans, rice, and pork; chicken would be endangered in Central America."

"I'm sorry Abuela, I know you like BBQ chicken. I will grab you a plate right now." Chico started to jog off.

In mid-stride, Abuela connected the cane to Chico's left temple. Chico was down and out. "Jason's mom is going to make my plate. Puta!"

Jason and Shiz attempted to recover Chico but stopped as soon as Ms. Perez raised her cane in their direction. "Leave him." Ms. Perez looked both boys in the eye and asked, "Why didn't you two, check on Abuela?"

"Abuela, real rap, we just came back from picking up some supplies for the block party." Shiz crossed his heart.

"You two are good boys. Stay sweet." Ms. Perez commenced to hobble off, then she turned towards Shiz. "O yea Sean, eat something. Your picture could get us funding from a third world country."

"For you Abuela, I will eat two Jason size plates," Shiz answered and she was on her way.

Jason turned to Shiz. "Are you going to help Chico up?"

Shiz looked at Chico, "Hell Naw, I'm not trying to look like Willie Lump Lump next to him. Plus, I got some business to handle. Excuse me my brother." Shiz stepped over his fallen combatant.

"What's good Shiz?" Turk inquired while shaking hands.

"Another day, another dollar." Shiz stepped back to check out his connect. Turk's attire screamed Harlemite; sporting white Airforce Ones, baggy blue jeans, white tee, Yankees fitted, topped with an iced-out chain and watch. "You know you look like a come up, with all that jewelry on."

"Unlike you, I'm squeezing with a license to carry."

"Whatever, you gonna let me shoot that…" Shiz became sidetracked by a blunt behind Turk's ear. "Am I on that blunt?"

"Can I get a plate from the block party?"

"We better hurry up and smoke then. Jason hasn't eaten in three hours."

Without hesitation, the blunt was sparked. Turk inhaled deeply, followed by a lip trembling slow exhale. After two more puffs, Turk passed the blunt to Shiz. He boldly inhaled, like a man ready to deep sea dive. Half of the blunt was smoke before Turk snatched it from Shiz's lips.

Turk snapped, "You smoking my shit like you on death row."

"You know I got the lungs of a whale."

"You should thank the Lord Trump isn't charging you for air Shamu." Turk inhaled twice, then said, "Before I get too stoned, let's get down to business."

Turk parked the blunt in the corner of his mouth, reached both hands into his pants, and removed half a pound of Canadian Jack Hairy. Swiftly, Shiz seized the bag of weed from Turk and placed it under his left armpit. Shiz dug into his right pocket and passed Turk a small fortune. Before Turk could begin counting, Shiz spat out, "I'm thirty dollars short."

"What?" Turk snatched the work, removed two big buds, then slammed the bag against Shiz chest. "You lucky I fuck with you; your miss management of funds is bad for business."

"Come on Turk, you the man out here."

"Dick eating don't pay the bills," Turk said seriously.

"Turk, you know I move that work. I flip at least twice a week." Shiz spoke with pride.

"Shiz that's chump change." Turk shrugged his shoulders, then continued to break Shiz down, "If you weren't funny as shit, we wouldn't be in business together."

"Really, my thousands of dollars is chump change?" Shiz asked as if he was doing it big.

Turk placed his right hand on Shiz's shoulder, removed the blunt from his lips, and bowed his head. "You cover my gas money and real hustlers hand me McDonald's franchise revenue." Turk slowly looked up at Shiz and passed the blunt, hoping it would soften the blow.

Shiz looked at Turk, like he just diagnosed him with cancer, "Sooo…"

Turk put a finger over Shiz lips. "Shhhhhh, just hit the weed and get your weight up," Turk attempted to soothe his dysfunctional client.

Shiz simultaneously sniffled, wiped his eyes and smoked. Shiz trembled and he quickly spun into an emotional breakdown. "This is too much to handle." Shiz launched the blunt to the ground.

Turk swooped down to recover the blunt. "Shiz you buggin, that's not a roach."

"Fuck that blunt dawg. I'm a two-bit hustler, with a habit like Whitney," Shiz whined loudly.

"Shiz you buggin. Let's hit the block party, so I can grab a plate and rout." Turk turned and walked away. After a few steps, Turk checked on Shiz. The depressed hustler was hugging the bag of weed like a pillow. "Put that weed away. I'm not trying to get booked, because you can't handle some tough love."

Shiz stashed the weed, attempted to get himself together, then ventured towards the block party. Turk and Shiz, approached a now conscious Chico and Jason.

Jason noticed Shiz's watery eyes. "You good Shiz?"

"I'm straight, my allergies are acting up." Shiz sniffled while looking in any direction but Jason's.

Jason continued his questioning, "Why are you lying? The last time your allergies were acting up Martin got canceled. So, what's really good?"

Shiz began to tear up again, "I loved Martin." Shiz planted his face into Jason's chest and wept loudly. Jason looked uncomfortable patting the back of Shiz's head.

Turk turned to Chico. "I can't go through this shit again. Walk me to get something to eat?" Chico nodded his head and they made their way towards the grills.

Jason grasped Shiz's shoulders and eased him away. "Shiz, what's really going on?"

Shiz used Jason's shirt to wipe his tears. Jason snatched it away before Shiz could blow on it. "Turk told me that I was only worth gas money. And, and, and......"

"And what?"

"And he said." Shiz swallowed hard, then continued, "Then he told me, 'I need to get my weight up'," Shiz whined, then planted his head back on Jason's chest.

A woman walking by talking on the phone, whispered into the receiver, "Gay pride is in full effect in North Philly."

Jason pushed Shiz away and told him, "Shiz, it ain't that bad. You still got the plug on the weed, you dress fly every day, and Kim is your girl."

"You're right Sweet Tooth," Shiz said while poking out his chest. "I'm smashing one of the finest chicks in Philly and all my Polo shirts are authentic."

Jason whispered to Shiz, "Come on cannon, straighten up and fly right. We're on the block."

"Alright, back up off me," Shiz barked, then pushed Jason away. "I don't play that soft shit."

Jason look to the sky, not knowing what to say. Once his gaze came out of the clouds, he spotted his mother traveling in his direction, with a husky plate of everything but swine. Jason was hypnotized by the plate, while Shiz was interested in a rack that wasn't on the menu.

Ms. Shabazz passed Jason the plate. But, before Jason could give thanks, Shiz was in her face. "Hey, Ms. Shabazz." Shiz arms flew open like a Venus flytrap and she walked right into his embrace. Jason's total focus was overwhelmed by the food, while Shiz monitored Jason and took pleasure in Ms. Shabazz embrace. "Damn, you smell like vanilla," fumbled from Shiz's lips in a sexual undertone.

"Sup," Jason mumbled, due to a chicken bone lodged in his mouth. Shiz quickly pulled away. A bare drumstick slowly fell from Jason's mouth, as he spotted Shiz's massive erection, trying to rip through his Seven Jeans. Jason began to tremble uncontrollably and the plate fumbled out of his hands. Jason roared, "What the fuck is wrong with you."

"Why are you going husky hulk on me?" Shiz asked, unaware of what was going on beneath his waistline.

"What the fuck is that?" Jason pointed at Shiz's crotch area.

"A blessing," Ms. Shabazz mumbled. Jason grabbed his afro, looking like he was going to remove a patch.

"Yo Jason, calm down," Shiz said tranquilly, like he had a solution to the problem. "Look Jason, I'm high."

"Well Shiz, I'm gonna detox all that shit."

Before Jason could charge, Ms. Shabazz cut him off and said, "Now Stinker, you know we don't curse. Let's go make salat and I'll make you another plate."

Jason turned childlike. "Mom, what did I tell you about calling me that name in front of my friends."

"Whatever, you're still my baby." Jason walked away, happily holding his mom, as if nothing just happened.

Shiz collapsed against the street light. "This weed got me open."

CHAPTER FIVE

The darkness of night caused the yellow streetlight to illuminate on the corner of Warnock and Brown Street. Chico and Shiz, hovered the curve with arms folded, as Jason pulled up from God knows where.

As soon as Jason exited the vehicle, Shiz began interrogating, "Where have you been for the past hour?" Jason proceeded to the passenger side of the vehicle and removed a two-foot-long cheesesteak.

"Really Jason, we got leftovers from the block party," Chico stated.

"Maxx's chicken cheesesteak was calling me. Plus, you know black people don't throw out leftovers. I will be eating barbecue for breakfast, lunch, dinner, and snacks."

"That's true and I will be sliding through for a plate or two," Shiz informed Jason, then pointed to Chico and himself. "Are you breaking bread on that chicken cheesesteak?"

"Yea, I got y'all." Then Jason leered at Shiz. "You lucky you're getting some, you rapist."

"Why are you defaming my character? You know weed is a natural aphrodisiac," Shiz responded.

"First and foremost, defamating is not a word. Secondly, my momma didn't ask for that, so that makes you a rapist."

"Chico, tell him to stop bringing up old shit. You're worse than those brothers still protesting for reparations."

"We do deserve reparations," Jason alleged while leading his crew to the trunk of his car.

"What we gonna do with reparation?" questioned Shiz. "Buy Cadillac's, Polo, and ball harder than Floyd Mayweather at a craps table."

Jason rubbed his chin, then spoke up, "It doesn't have to be money, it could be free education or property."

Chico spazzed out, "Fuck y'all Roots moment." Jason and Shiz, gave Chico their undivided attention.

Shiz responded, "Shorty Doo Wop, what do you know about Roots?"

"I know." Chico placed a hand over his heart, then continued, "It should have been more scenes in Africa, at the beginning of Roots."

Jason looked puzzled. "Why?"

"Roots is the only nude flick Abuela owns. Yi Mean?" Chico informed his friends.

Shiz laughed hysterically. "Shit done hit the fan. Chico jerking off to Alex Haley's relatives. You won't be looking at my family pictures."

"No one wants to see your family's mugshots in orange jumpsuits," Chico opposed, then turned towards Jason. "Big homie, tell me you weren't digging those chocolate dipped nipples, straight from the motherland?" Jason looked in the air and whistled. Chico flung his hands in the air and screamed, "Forget y'all."

After laughing at Chico's pain, the crew went to town on the two-foot-long sandwich. In under 10 minutes, the food was gone, and the itis had kicked in. Shiz was down, but not out and decided to roll up. In less than four minutes a blunt was broke down, licked, stuffed, twisted, and ready for blastoff.

"How can you smoke after eating? I got the itis to the 2nd power." Jason yawned while stretching.

With the blunt dangling from his lips, he mumbled "Rolling up after eating is the bomb, like a hot wash rag after sex,"

Shiz straightened up as Kim's white Range Rover came to a stop. With zero indecision, Shiz made his way to the driver side of the SUV. The tinted driver window rolled down and Kim's Tianjin beauty was revealed. Long black curls fell over her honey brown shoulders, light lip gloss covered her thin lips, and her black halter top covered just enough for Kim not to be arrested for indecent exposure. Shiz put the blunt behind his ear, then stuck his head in the window and began slowly kissing his Asian craving.

"Hey Shiz!" Kim's transsexual entourage of four greeted him in unison. If you didn't know them personally, you could get caught in the wrong, like believing RuPaul could be your next baby momma.

Shiz imitated Wendy Williams, "How you doin?" As usual, Kim's entourage acted like audience members and returned the greeting. After the playful greeting, Shiz got right to business, "What's the order for today?"

"What's on the menu?" asked Kim's friend in the passenger seat.

"We got weed, water, and Xanies."

"Y'all need to have combo's like McDonald's. Like, a number two would come with four Xanies and a bag of bud." Two of the transsexuals in the backseat gave each other a high five.

Another passenger, in the back seat, followed up, "I would be like 'give me a number two and super-size that bag of bud'." The entourage shared high fives and laughs.

"Maybe I will do that," Shiz lied.

"Do that honey," stated one of the passengers, with more snaps than a poetry crowd.

"Stop playing around, he gotta make my money," Kim snapped on her posse.

"Kim, you need to put him on 11th and Chestnut. Those closet boys would eat him up," one said quickly.

"Mo money, mo money, mo money!" Another passenger encouraged.

"Kim is right, I got to get this money."

"You know we just playing." One popped his lips and continued, "Let us get $200 worth of that funky town and 20 blues." They scrambled their money together and passed it to Kim.

"Don't forget about me," Kim said seductively, as she passed the money to Shiz.

"How could I do that Goldie?" Shiz said jokingly and made his way to Jason.

One of Kim's entourage, in the back-passenger seat, began pointing at Jason. "Doesn't that husky bull look like Ab Lava, from Major Figure?" Before anyone could respond, the groupie continued,

"Girl, I'm about to crack." The window rolled down and the seducer's head popped out. "Hey Ab, I'm Keisha."

"Keyshawn, I'm not the one. I would be disrespectful, but I'm on my dean," Jason spoke with pride.

"Oh, you a gangster ockie. Malcolm X could have used you. Do you want to be my body guard?" The seducer bit the tip of his long thin index finger.

As soon as Shiz made it to the curve, Jason snapped, "Your company is being reckless and it needs to roll."

"Don't be like that Biggie," Jason's groupie informed him, then began singing loudly, "Biggie give me one damn chance. Biggie Biggie give me one damn chance."

Chico hugged the streetlight, trying to hold himself up from dying laughing. "Jason you got a chubby chaser."

The seducer popped his lips and continued to serenade Jason, "Shiz, why he actin shy like he doesn't want to taste my sweet nectar." Jason's stomach caved in and a melting pot came up. "Biggie, that ain't a good look for you. We can talk once you clean up."

Shiz pointed towards the perpetrator. "Yo Kim, kill that shit."

Kim turned towards her thirsty passenger, "Bitch, sit back and roll up my window. You acting thirsty like you fresh out of boot camp."

Shiz patted Jason's back, while requesting twenty Xanies. Jason complied and passed the pills off. The excretion on the curve caught Shiz's attention and he began to shake his head. "I was wondering who ate all the watermelon. No mercy for the seeds, huh?"

Jason attempted to punch Shiz's leg. Shiz dodged the punch, then made his way towards Kim. The transaction was made and Shiz examined his lover. "Baby, you know I want you by my side all the time, like my forty-five. Why don't you ever chill with me on the block?"

"Really Sean?" Kim looked around, then looked at Shiz like he was stupid. "You think I wear these Red Bottom to please the hood?"

"Preach," the entourage sung in harmony.

"You can sport some Jordan's and tights. You know I like it when you dress down." Shiz nodded his head, hoping she would follow suit.

"Not gonna happen Sean. Anyway, that's not the reason, why I'm not posting on the block." Kim looked away.

"Then what's the reason baby?"

"While you're on the block, you're at work. And Asian's work behind bulletproof glass in North Philly. Yi mean?"

"Baby ain't shit...."

Kim placed a finger over his lips. "Whatever Sean, someone just got killed on 10th & Poplar yesterday."

"Baby, niggas always getting smoked around there," he said jokingly.

"And they say silence is golden." Kim chuckled and shook her head.

"Kim, I'll let you hold my gun. We can be like Bonnie and Clyde in these streets."

"Working men are so sexy," Kim pecked him on the lips. "Call me when you get off." Kim sped from the curve.

Shiz looked in the direction of her tail lights. "She's just in a rush to get back to me. Yi mean?"

"You don't have to explain to us, convince your crusty ass lips," Chico cracked.

Shiz noticed Major doing the backstroke under a Ford F-150. "Chico, get Major before the cops find out who sold him that wet."

Major was yelling orders to an imaginary battalion, "Grunts, make it ashore and give them hell."

"Lord help these Vets." Chico jogged off to handle his business.

Jason turn to Shiz. "That dust juice ain't for the weak minded."

"Your blues ain't no better. Remember when I popped those zanies and bought Kim all that Victoria Secret? Man, I almost fucked up my re-up money. I can't believe those draws cost so much." Shiz shook his head, then continued. "I had to sell my food stamps just to bounce back."

Jason judged Shiz's ethics, "You suppose to use that EBT money to purchase cold food."

Shiz shrugged his shoulders. "When money is low, everything must go. Yi mean?"

Major's shouting caused Jason and Shiz to break their neck in his direction. Major was haul assing in the direction of 10th Street. "Not today Charlie; I will die before I become a Prisoner of War."

Chico slowly approached his comrades, with a knot on his forehead and car oil stains on his tan Dickies. Jason and Shiz shared a pre-story laugh.

Chico began acting out the story. "That fool pulled me under the truck, headbutted me and took off running."

Jason decided to drop a jewel on his injured companion, "Chico, all money, ain't good money."

"Yea and all money ain't guaranteed like Major's disability check," Chico countered. Jason looked at Chico harshly.

Shiz put his hand on Jason's shoulder. "Don't be so hard on the young whippersnapper. It's hard giving up guaranteed money. That's like letting go of your head doctor for a potential Wifey."

"The Holy Quran says, I shouldn't deal with idiots," Jason recited.

Chico folded his arms. "Whatever dawg. You're in the same moral free industry as us."

"I'm…" Jason paused as he peeped a white and black guy strolling in their direction; wearing glasses, suits, ties, and book bags. Chico and Shiz turned to see what caught Jason's attention.

"What's up with these cats?" Shiz stated, then turned to Jason, "If they had bow ties and bean pies, I would think they were one of your ockies."

"Why do you swear I know every brother with a bow tie and kufi?" Jason responded.

Before Shiz could crack another joke, the black gentleman cut into the conversation, "How good has Jehovah been to you brothers?"

"I'm sure Allah has been blessing my man with those racks," Shiz said while patting Jason on his back.

The white witness formed prayer hands. "Well, donations should be no issue."

Chico's spider sense was screaming. "When did Jehovah's Witness start hustling the word after dark and asking for donations?"

The white gentleman reached into his suit jacket. "Check out this pamphlet and…." Swiftly, a nine-millimeter was removed from his suit. The Warnock Crew jumped back with hands raised. "Don't move or you'll be losing more than money tonight."

MICHAEL HIGGINS JR.

His partner in crime removed a snub-nose three-fifty-seven from his suit. "Move slowly toward the silver Marauder and put your hands on the roof."

"A fella, I just wash my car, don't let dirty bull touch it." Jason nodded toward Chico.

Chico banged his fist on the roof of Jason's car. "We getting robbed and you thinking about your resale value."

Jason turned towards the black gunman. "Come on my brother, my momma needs this money or she'll have to return to stripping."

"Do I look like I give a fuck. Now put your hands on the car fat boy." Jason followed the black gunman's order. "Bro hit those pockets, so we can bounce."

"You heard the man, pass off that watch, or this gun will be putting you on a weight loss program." Jason removed the watch from his wrist and passed it off to the white gunman. The gunman, pressed the muzzle of the 9mm to the back of Jason's head, as he snatched the watch from his grasp; then removed the content from Jason's pockets.

The white guy eyeballed Chico's neck, "What'cha got around your neck Pedro?" He leaned in to take a closer look. "Naw you can keep that whack ass Rosary."

"Stop disrespecting my Jesus piece Puta."

"You disrespecting Jesus, by hanging him from a beaded shoestring, with no VVS diamonds." The gunman pushed his 9mm against Chico's head, then ransacked his pockets.

While searching Shiz's pockets, Shiz decided to speak up, "Take the money and the gun, but leave the blunt. I'm gonna need something to smoke after this shit."

After emptying Shiz pockets and grabbing the blunt from behind his ear, the gunman backed away. "Now, get on the ground and count to 50."

They followed the order and began counting. The robbers sprinted off. Chico let them get a head start, then he was off to the races.

Jason got up and noticed Shiz had an issue counting pass 20. Jason pulled Shiz up by his belt. "They getting away stupid," Jason yelled, then took off running.

Chico got within twenty yards, when he noticed the white robber turn, extend his firearm, and showcase the blue flame from the muzzle. Chico dove between park cars, as thunderous gunfire erupted. Seconds later, a car began screeching away and Chico scrambled to the middle of the streets. The assailants pilled from the curve in a red Monte Carlo, with a bumper sticker that read 'Holy Rollers'.

"Say no more." Chico engulfed the details of the vehicle, stood, and repeated, "Say no more."

CHAPTER SIX

Jason and Shiz posted on the corner, with their heads on a swivel, and hands not far from a burner. Two weeks ago, Chico was put on punishment, and the operation now had a major void. Sherm heads, acted like children experiencing a shitty Christmas, when they heard there was no dippers for sell.

Jason's mean mug evaporated, when he spotted Chico on Abuela's front step. Jason tapped Shiz. "Chico on the step."

"Let's see how bad Abuela lumped him up," Shiz responded.

"Have some compassion, that's our young bull."

The two-man crew made their way towards their M.I.A. companion. Chico sat on the front step, with his arms folded on his lap and head down. Shiz and Jason stopped a foot away from their colleague.

Jason placed a hand on Chico's shoulder. "You good?"

Chico slowly raised his head, revealing a fading black eye. "Damn!" Jason and Shiz, flinched like they were preparing for the punch.

"Your eye wouldn't look so bad, if you weren't so high yellow," Shiz informed Chico.

Jason connected a slap to the back of Shiz's head. "How are you doing Chico?"

"As good as a 17-year-old can be, with a lack of freedom."

"Damn Chico, she like a hundred years old, you couldn't weave her jab?" Shiz imitated Ali's roper dope.

"If you think that's bad, my back could make homegirl from '12 Years a Slave' cringe."

"Did Abuela beat you with an extension cord?" Jason asked. Chico slowly nodded his head. "Abuela practicing Willy Lynch's slave breaking methods. Stay strong my brother."

"I'm not running away," Chico sounded humbler than a field hand on a water break.

"Cut the bull shit, are we getting our water boy back or what?" asked Shiz.

"Yea, but first I have to finish writing the whole Old Testament of the Bible."

"You should pray for Moses to set you free," Shiz suggested.

"Shut up," Jason ordered Shiz, then turned to Chico. "Thanks for getting our stuff back, but why didn't you tell us, you were going to ride on those clowns?"

"You think I didn't want to smack somebody with the burner?" Shiz backslapped his hand.

Chico's demeanor went arctic cold, "Fuck what both of y'all talking about, I do my dirt, how I do my dirt. And I don't like too many witnesses." Chico looked at his comrades to confirm they caught his drift.

Shiz bust out laughing. "Where did you learn that, Serial Killing for Dummies?"

"Naw, Rell," Chico informed Shiz.

Shiz immediately stopped laughing and cleared his throat. Rell was a respected hitman in his youth, before he mastered the world of money laundering. Chico continued, "What happened after the block party, ain't happening twice."

"I'm with you Popi, we should holla at Chip," Jason encouraged.

Shiz folded his arms. "Here we go again with this Chip shit. Homeboy been locked down longer than Nelson Mandela, he needs to be thinking about Medicare."

"Him getting locked up isn't a bad thing in our case. Chip was a top dog around here before getting sentenced. Plus, being locked up with like-minded criminals could have only sharpened his game," Jason philosophized.

"Jason and I are down with hollering at Chip. Are you going to be a team player or Allen Iverson at the point?" Chico questioned Shiz.

"You insane for even speaking that blaspheme. AI is the team." Shiz performed a crossover then a fadeaway.

Chico leered at Shiz. "Fuck that, are you down to be coached or what?"

Shiz slowly applauded. "You could have won an Oscar for that speech, my soul moved."

"Shiz!" screamed Chico and Jason.

"I'm down."

Before they could shake on it, Abuela swung open the front door. Jason and Shiz jumped back, then turned and ran.

"Jesus, who told you, you could have company?" Abuela questioned with more flare than Rosy Perez.

"Abuela en el exterior…" Before Chico could give his defense, she connected her cane to Chico's left shoulder. Jason and Shiz prayed for their compadre, as his scream echoed through Richard Allen Projects.

CHAPTER SEVEN

A month passed since Abuela's public assault. Chico was granted freedom once again, but things were different now. Like a franchising company, Chip organized, trained, and mentored the young tycoons. First and foremost, Chip had the boys stashing their inventory at a neighbor's house, who didn't have any habits, except drug money. He made them invest together, so everyone could make the same profit and prices would go down, due to copping more weight. Their hours of operation were now from ten to ten. Lunch breaks were incorporated to keep the team mentally sharp.

The crew now had assigned roles to play in the drug trade. Jason was the gunman, because of his history of putting his mother's boyfriends out of commission. Chico handled money transaction, due to his anti-social attitude and fast counting ability. A young honest kid, name Keem, was hired to handle drug transactions. Shiz initially refused his role as a lookout, believing it was a flunky's position. Chip explained, that he was too much of a social butterfly to conduct drug transactions and shook like a man with Parkinson's behind the trigger.

Chip made them listen to the 'Art of War', 'Book of 5 Rings', 'How to Read People like a Book', and 'The Richest Man in Babylon' audiobooks. Jason was instructed to go to a shooting range once a week; to master handling, aiming, and discharging his firearm. He was trained to do all handling of his firearm with a glove, rag, or other object, just in case the gun had to be tossed. Jason's other responsibility, was to make the runs for the re-up and collect funds when the income exceeded five hundred dollars. The group learned nonverbal hand signals and body language; to communicate business transaction and other signals to keep each other safe. The mastermind taught them how to look incognito on the block and to trust their gut feeling when it came to who not to serve. The for-sale stash was placed on car tires or hidden within Jason's view. Sales were now made in the middle of the block, instead of on the corner.

Chip took the most time schooling Shiz. The first habit Chip broke, was Shiz's 24/7 smoking routine. After two hours of convincing Shiz that, weed doesn't give him Spider senses and he's losing money because of his frivolous smoking habit, Shiz finally complied with the order to only smoke during his free time. The second practice that Shiz had to remove, was being a social butterfly on the clock; because it could leave his team locked up, stuck up, or bodied. Chip explained, the importance of telling people that didn't fit the bill of a potential customer to kick rocks. Lastly, Shiz was to keep the drama away from their operation, like breaking up baby momma fights to getting naked sherm heads doing yoga away from the operation.

The last and most important subject, Chip schooled them on, was the real nature of the dope game. "This is a loser's game. Stack your money and find other ways to make money outside of this lifestyle. It doesn't matter if it's investing your time and money in education, business, a craft or a trade. That was my downfall years ago, I didn't invest my time outside of the dope game. So, when the man caught me with the work, I had no alibi for my lawyer to work with. The best advice I could give y'all, is to stay low key and invest some time and money outside the dope game." After a month of functioning under Chip's New World Order, their operation looked like a living masterpiece.

Shiz was the first to notice it was time for their second break. Shiz popped his collar in Chico's direction, Chico nodded and made his way towards Jason; who was sitting in a lawn chair in front of his house. Keem went home to play NBA 2K. Like clockwork, Jason's mom came out with three lunch bags. Chico and Shiz sat on each side of Jason, as Ms. Shabazz squirted hand sanitizer in her employer's hands.

"Stinker, remember to tuck that paper towel into your shirt. I'm not trying to be scrubbing no more mustard stains out of your Dickies," Ms. Shabazz ordered, with a hand on her hip.

"Ms. Shabazz, I will make sure Stinker follows your order," Shiz said with a big smile.

Jason jabbed Shiz in the shoulder, then turned to his mom. "Mom, what did I say about calling me that?"

"You cool enough to be my stinker in the house, but outside you want to act brand new. Boy bye," she said, then sauntered off.

"Chico, how are our profits looking today?" asked Shiz.

"Mucho fedia!"

Shiz tossed his arms in the air. "Telemundo, ain't no caption beneath your chin. Speak English my man, English."

"$640 apiece," Chico replied.

"Why am I taking a loss for our eating habit?" Shiz asked his crew.

Jason answered, "Because it's your weed connect that keeps our chef happy. Plus, every morning, you slide through and treat my mom's breakfast or our leftovers like a buffet."

"True," Chico cosigned.

"Telemundo, you suppose to have my back. Mi casa su casa my nigga," Shiz supposed, then stood. "A water ice would go perfect with this sandwich. I'll be back."

"Don't lollygag in there. We back to work in ten minutes," Chico ordered and Shiz responded with a thumb in the air as he walked off. Chico turned to Jason, "Shiz's water ice habit is almost heavier than his weed habit."

Jason nodded in agreement. While raising his sandwich for a bite, Jason paused and gazed at Chico with confusion.

Chico noticed Jason's odd stare and confronted him, "Why are you looking at me, like I gave the verdict to the O.J. Simpson trial?"

"You know we have been hustling together for about two years now," said Jason.

"And?" Chico responded, then took a sip of his grape hug bottle.

"You know, I break bread with my momma when my funds are proper, that is my habit, Ya dig?"

Chico coughed into his fist, "Momma's boy."

"My point is, you don't have a drug habit, you can't cross Abuela's doorway with groceries or clothes without being questioned; and to my knowledge, you don't own shit. No disrespect."

"None taken."

"So, what do you do with your money?"

Without hesitation, Chico replied, "I pay myself a king's wage, as you should."

"If all Americans were tightwads like you, capitalism would be a thing of the past."

Chico gave a head nod towards the street. "A Jason, Jamaica's most wanted is heading our way."

Cherie's grandma looked both ways, three times, before crossing the street. Once she made it to Jason's house, Chico got right to business, "We on break, I…"

"Lazy Americans," disgust was evident in her thick Jamaican accent. "In my country, we worked part-time jobs on our breaks."

"How much do you want; I will bring it to you after my break," Chico asked, then took a sip from his hug bottle.

"Why didn't one of you idiots stop me before I crossed the street?"

"You got here so fast we didn't have a chance," Jason said.

"I didn't expect you to move, egg shape boy. I was talking to the border jumper."

"I'm sorry," Chico apologized.

"Lazy boy, bring me two 20's sacks," she ordered, then journeyed home.

Minutes later, Shiz returned, with a white Styrofoam cup, filled to the hilt with mango water ice and a plastic spoon. Shiz put the water ice in Jason's face, then quickly retracted it.

"You lucky I didn't lick that jawn," said Jason.

Chico lusted over the water ice in Shiz's hand. "That jawn do look good. Can you hold me down with a mango water ice when we get off?"

"As long as you have a dollar, penny-pincher," Shiz picked up his sandwich and began to demolish it.

"Really Shiz?" Chico responded.

"Popi, those mangos ain't free."

Jason cut in, "Discuss the issue after work, it's time to punch the clock."

"Where Chip at?" Shiz inquired.

"You know he visits his probation officer every Tuesday," answered Jason.

"You believe that shit?" Shiz twisted his lips.

"Sherlock Public Homes, what's the four one one?" Chico cocked his head to the left and got ready for another one of Shiz's crazy theories.

Shiz looked over both shoulders, before speaking his mind, "Chip probably goes to a head doctor, to get over all the gay shit he been through in prison. I hope they fix him; I haven't been in the weight room in a while."

Jason and Chico looked at each other, then shook their head. Jason replied, "On that note, let's get back to the money."

Shiz made his way to the corner. Keem exited his house and headed towards Shiz, to crack a couple of jokes before the operation got too busy. Jason slouched in his chair, with a newspaper on his lap, that concealed a three eighty. Chico went to the stash, removed Ms. Marley's order, and made his way to her house.

She opened the door as Chico approached, "Lazy boy, you could learn something from your Mexican cousins. Carlos only takes breaks on Sunday to pay tithes and play soccer."

"Well I'm Dominican and my closest relatives are African, so that means I will be on color people time and demand breaks."

"Nuh pay yuh nuh mind, yuh a bagga mouth." Patwa flew from her mouth so fast, Chico couldn't keep up.

"I'm on the clock, here is your green." He passed her two sacks. She snatched the bud and pressed it to her nostrils. She smiled with satisfaction, then placed the weed in her bra and removed forty dollars from the same place.

Chico grabbed the money and was about to leave, when she spoke up, "Yuh light up di grades?" She asked with a smile on her face.

"No thanks, I don't do drugs."

Her smile flipped upside down. "Mi don't do drug neither." She placed one hand behind the door, then spat out, "Yuh a eediat." The door was slammed in Chico's face. He pocketed her money and was off to work.

In no time, Chico had a swarm of customers and Chico excelled at handling the transaction. Keem mastered both serving and communicating through hand signals faster than a shark learns to kill. Jason kept a hawk eye on the operation. Shiz kept his head on a swivel, watching for anything alarming.

"What the fuck?" spiraled from Shiz's lips, as an older white man in a trench coat, headed his way. Shiz yelled out, "Fuck it's hot." Chico took a walk, while Shiz nervously examined his water ice, to avoid eye contact with the weirdo.

"Hey sport," the stranger greeted Shiz with a thick southern drawl.

"My man, you'll never make it on 60 Minutes shooting around here. I would be surprised if you made it on Snap Chat."

The stranger cracked up. "Slick, I'm not into that Columbine shit. I got them things for sale though." The stranger made a hand jester as if he were pulling a trigger.

Shiz looked the stranger in the matrix jacket up and down. "Them things?"

"Yea, them things." He looked over both shoulders and Shiz did the same. The mystery man unbuttoned his jacket and unveiled a gun store. "I got sawed offs, nines, three-fifty-sevens, three-eighties, thirty-eights, forties, forty-fours, forty-fives, and a Mack. I also do special orders for bullets and rocket launchers. You look like a bow and arrow man. I got one on my back, do you want to see?"

"I'm cool on that Rambo shit."

"Alright bro, fuck the bow, what about the rest of my merchandise?"

Shiz rubbed his palms together with excitement. "What's good with that sawed off?"

"It's a twelve-gauge Mossberg 500, with a pistol grip. This slugger holds five shells, with one in the chamber. The asking price is three hundred dollars and I'll even throw in a box of shells."

"That jawn is steep. My man Miz bought his shotty for an ounce and a half of regular weed. You're talking exotic weed prices." Shiz rubbed his chin, then continued, "Do you smoke? I'll trade you for that jawn, I got the best weed in the city."

Instantly, the man closed his jacket. "Why does every weed man say that. Anyway, I don't use or sell that poison. Money is the only high you can offer me," the salesman alleged while buttoning up his showcase.

"Slide through next week, maybe we can talk numbers."

"Alright Bro." The man strolled off and sung out, "Stop the violence and increase the peace."

Shiz watched the salesman walk off, then he coughed loudly three times, to signal Chico to get back to work. Shiz monitored Chico, until he noticed a puddle of water trembling in the street. Seconds later, Shiz heard the chick, from the intro of all Maybach Music songs, echoing through the hood. Rick Ross's latest street banger, had car and house windows trembling. Bama's 63 navy blue drop top Impala, screeched around the corner, on 24-inch chrome rims.

Shiz sprinted to the middle of the street and screamed, "Pull your drawlin ass over and kill that radio."

Bama followed Shiz's order, then hopped out of the vehicle. He shook his head back and forth to loosen up his dreads. "What up folk." Bama's smile revealed a rose gold grill.

"You drawlin, is not what's up. We told you to turn down your radio around here. We're moving dope out here, not competing with a Power House concert."

"You know I don't remember nothing when I'm on those blues. Just keep me posted and I'll see what I can do." Bama slapped Shiz's on the arm and kept it moving.

Bama approached Chico, with a handshake. "Sup Folk."

Chico left him hanging. "Bama, why do we always have to tell you to turn down your radio?"

"Look shorty, my life is a party and Philly invited." Bama started to Milly Rock.

"Your party is going to put my crew in an eight by ten, Ya dig?" Chico responded without a playful bone in his body.

"My bad Folk, let me get four blues and a dipper," Bama said while removing some money from his pocket.

Chico looked towards Bama's drop top, which was still running. "You know someone could jump in your car and vamoose?"

Bama turned around, exposing an erection, caused by a forty-round clip in his nine-millimeter. "Someone could try, but I'll be helping them climb that stairway to heaven." Bama gestured with his hands that he had heard enough, "Fuck that scary talk folk. Grab my work, so I can put my dreads in the wind."

Chico didn't respond to his foolishness. Instead, he made a few hand signals and Keem quickly made the transaction. Bama engulfed the blue pills, then sparked the embalming fluid soaked cigarette. With no rap, Bama put up a peace sign and strolled to his car. Bama slightly turned up his radio and drove off.

Not even a second later, Shiz's Spidey sense went off. When he turned toward 11th Street, a strange dude dressed like the black version of Malibu's Most Wanted, was doing the Ace Ventura walk in Shiz's direction.

Shiz cut into the stranger immediately, "What's good."

"What up Money, where the weed at?" The oddball asked.

"I don't think they sell weed around here, but let me ask my young bull," Shiz turned to Chico and yelled, "Yurp!"

Chico jogged over, knowing something was up. Shiz's smirk and wildly scratching his chest let Chico know that this character had to go. Chico's half ass smile confirmed it was on.

"Como esta?" Chico asked Shiz.

"Telemundo, this con man," Shiz cleared his throat, then continued, "I mean kind man, is looking for weed."

"Where did you look already?" Chico questioned him, while scratching his chin.

"This my first stop."

"You should check 18th & Montgomery or Broad & Market," Chico referred.

The stranger looked puzzled. "People sell weed around city hall and the police district?"

"I don't believe so, but they can tell you where to get some," answered Chico.

"Someone told me that Warnock Street got that fire."

"They lied to you. All we're known for is robbing around here." Shiz cracked his knuckles. The stranger's head snapped in Shiz's direction.

"How much money you trying to spend?" Chico asked slyly. The man's head swung in Chico's direction. Shiz tugged on his jeans pocket and the undercover skedaddled.

Chico and Shiz laughed, until they observed Cherie pull up, with Chip in the passenger seat. Cherie headed home and Chip headed towards his mentees.

Chip shook his head in disapproval, "Y'all lollygagging, scaring off customers. Where do they do that at?"

"Naw Chip, we were messing with this undercover. You could have got down, if you were here," Shiz replied.

"Why would I want to fuck with the man? I'm on probation, you lucky I'm banging with y'all." Chip paused to collect his thoughts, then continued, "A man that makes money off honey, doesn't fuck with the bees. And a drug dealer, who doesn't want to be a victim of a sting operation, would do the same."

"You right, I…"

Chip cut off Shiz, "What's that?" Chip pointed at Shiz's water ice. "You running to the store on shift?"

"Naw O.G., this my recipe."

"I'm surprised your mom allows you in the kitchen," Chip joked.

"I got that work, fuck with me," Shiz promoted his water ice with confidence, then removed a spoon from his back pocket and passed it to Chip.

Chip examined the spoon. "I guess it's not weird, that you walk around with an extra spoon in your back pocket."

"Just try me out."

Chip dug the spoon into the water ice, closed his eyes, and prepared for the worst taste known to man. But the counter punch he received sent his taste buds into ecstasy. "That jawn is crack." Chip snatched the cup from Shiz's hand. "You don't need this young bull, stay focus."

"What I say Chico, jailhouse strength," Shiz said, while watching the ex-con demolish the water ice.

"This jawn is off the hook. If you sold water ice, I would buy from you," Chip confirmed.

"With what money? You ain't got no job and I don't have an EBT machine." Shiz scratched his head. "I could download an EBT app though."

"My girl would hold me down," Chip informed Shiz.

"You mooching off my girl?" Shiz asked defensively.

"Shiz, she doesn't know your name," Chico enlighten his thirsty amigo.

"Chico's right, she calls you, 'that skinny bull on the corner'."

"You're right, bros before hoes." As the words left Shiz's mouth, a fist connected to Shiz's mid-section. The impact sat Shiz on his back pocket. Shiz waved a hand in the air, "Have you ever heard of a figure of speech?"

"Just focus on the water ice, ya dig?" Chip glared at Shiz.

"How you just hit me, I believe water ice is the topic of the day." Shiz braced his stomach, as he slowly made it back to his feet. "I'm gonna holla at June Bug, maybe I can set up a water ice stand in front of his crib." Shiz stepped off to talk business. Chip felt honorable, helping Shiz realize another path of making ends meet beyond the dope game.

Shiz crossed his heart before ringing June Bug's doorbell. He didn't seek Jesus to help him with this business venture, he prayed to God no pest attacked him when June Bug opened the door. Shiz ringed the doorbell and stepped back. Seconds later, June Bug snatched open the door. Shiz's nose flared, as he scrutinized June Bug scratching his ass. "What up ock?" June Bug extended his un-sanitized hand.

"Are you serious June Bug? I just saw you scratching your ass. I'm good on the physical greetings."

June Bug chuckled. "I didn't think you peeped that."

"We less than two feet away from each other. How could I not peep, you reaching around and digging in your ass?"

"You always keep it a bean, that's why I fuck with you." June Bug stepped forward and planted his funky hand on Shiz left shoulder.

Shiz Harlem Shaked the hand off his shoulder, then got right to business, "The reason why I'm not gonna two piece you for that shameless shit, is because I need a favor."

"Cool, let's talk in my office." June Bug moved to the side to let Shiz come in.

Shiz looked beyond his host and noticed a mouse checking who was at the door. Shiz shook his head back and forth. "It won't take that long. I want to set a water ice stand in front of your crib. I'll give you ten dollars a day."

"That sounds good, but let me talk with my business partner," June Bug went in the house and closed the door. Three minutes later, he returned.

"Is your mom down or what?" Shiz asked, with as much seriousness as he could muster up.

"My business partner and I, agree to receive a dub sack of weed, every morning." June Bug countered.

"I don't know why I believed y'all would prefer money over weed." Shiz popped his self in the head.

"Yea, I don't know why you would believe that. We get checks around here. And now, we don't even need to buy weed." June Bug began doing the Cabbage Patch, while continuing his demands, "Your rent is due every morning before you start. You not going to hit us with, 'we trying to burn you, because you high'."

"It's a deal."

"Let's shake on it." June bug extended his hand once again.

Shiz's top lip covered his nostrils, as he examined the extended hand. "How bout we just bow like the Asians do?" Shiz performed prayer hands, bowed, then bounced.

CHAPTER EIGHT

Three weeks had passed since Chip inspired Shiz to sell water ice. Shiz proposed the new enterprise to Chico and Jason, and they agreed a water ice stand could be a good way to stay incognito, while watching the drug trade. That day, Shiz invested his drug money into his new revenue stream. Once the water ice stand was up and going, Shiz marketed his product by handing out testers. Majority of the testers immediately purchased more water ice. The compliments he received brought his self-esteem to a new level. A lot of the kids in the neighborhood asked for chips and popcorn, and Shiz used his EBT card to purchase what the kids desired. When Adults began asking for bottled water, he put his EBT card to work again, and profits increased. Shiz was climbing Maslow's Hierarchy to self-actualization, finding joy in inventing unique water ice flavors and the city paid him for his genius. The business grew rapidly, requiring him to hire a young girl from the neighborhood named Sheena and purchase another ice box to store his new flavors. Chico became a disciple of the movement, promoting the water ice stand to the drug clientele. Shiz's water ice stand received great reviews on Yelp and Google. The streets were saying, "Weed and water ice, belong together, like a Big Mac and fries."

The day at hand, was going great for both operations. Chico and Keem, were moving clients along with no issues. Shiz and Sheena, were serving double scoops at the speed of light. As of lately, Jason kept a sketch pad and pencil in hand. Jason was restless and decided to holla at Shiz, since he didn't have a mob of kids around his stand.

Shiz noticed Jason coming his way with a newspaper under his armpit and sketch pad in his right hand. "What's good?"

Jason shook his head, "I can't call it."

Shiz locked eyes on the back of Jason's sketch pad, which was pressed against his thigh. "Doodling again?"

"I'm not doodling; I'm working on my mom's budget."

"I guess your color pencils are for pie charts?" Shiz asked and Jason looked around to avoid the comment. "If we were playing Bull Shit, you would be picking up the whole deck."

"Whatever."

Shiz twisted his lips. "Show me you're not sketching stick figures and I'll leave you alone."

"No."

"Why not?"

"Because, you're not supportive of my dreams," Jason believed.

"Really Jason," Shiz placed a hand over his heart. "I'm Mr. Supportive."

"What about the time I was trying to lose weight?"

"You brought those jokes upon yourself. You could have jogged in sweatpants, a tracksuit, or a black two-piece trash bag. But no, you had to sport a black and white one-piece spandex."

"That outfit was resistance free and you know my thighs be rubbing."

"You looked like a baby killer whale." Shiz laughed.

"That's the support I'm talking about."

"Well, I guess I'm the one that needs the support; because I get weak when I see stupid shit." Shiz paused, then looked up and down Brown Street. "Enough about you Free Willy, where is that jive throwback ex-con Chip? It's six something and he's not back yet."

"You know where he goes every Tuesdays."

Shiz slowly recited, "I don't know shit."

"What don't you know?" Jason cocked his head to the side, waiting for the logic of a man that lacked it.

"Word on the street is, Tuesday is International Informant Check-In Day."

"What?" Jason blinked hard and took a moment to process Shiz's statement. "So, you believe Chip is a rat, even though he improved our drug operation and motivated you to start a legal business?"

"Think about it my brother." Shiz tapped his index finger against his temple, then continued, "First and foremost, you saw American Made. Secondly, what ex-con doesn't sport a white beater in the summer?" Shiz hammered his fist on the freezer box. "Guilty!"

"Maybe he doesn't want the world to know he's packing heat."

"Or maybe he's strapped with a wire."

"Shiz, he's not a rat, I looked up his court docket online."

"Jason, he in too deep. You down with tossing J Reid in a pool?"

Jason performed a three-sixty turn. "What pool? We in the projects."

"Alright, plan B, put him in the full Nelson and I'll frisk him." Jason looked at Shiz like he was stupid. "What?"

"Yurp!" Jason waved over Chico.

Chico strolled over. "Talk to me."

"Your man." Jason pointed at Shiz, then continued, "Believes Chip is an informant and wants me to put him in a Full Nelson, so he can pat Chip down."

"I don't have time for this shit." Chico looked down the street and spotted a customer coming. "I'm back to work, here come Sleepy."

Instead of Sleepy crossing the street to get served, he approaches Jason. "If it ain't the overweight hustler."

"Sleepy, cop and roll like Sunoco," ordered Jason.

"You look like you went down from a D to a C cup. I didn't know men paid for boob reductions." Shiz giggled at Sleepy's humor.

"Keep coming at me like I'm sweet and I'll wire your jaw." Jason clenched his teeth.

Sleepy approached Jason, poked him in the chest, then pushed his chest together like he was fluffing a pillow. "Dog your chest should be on a Sealy's commercial." Sleepy nodded off on Jason's chest. Jason shoved his head away. "Momma, I dropped out. Let me sleep."

"Yo," Shiz yelled. "Sleepy you drawlin; cop your shit and skedaddle."

Sleepy did an about face, drifted into the street and almost got ran over.

Chico cut right to the chase as Sleepy approached, "Six blues, right?"

"And a Jason size bag of bud." Sleepy nodded off twice, while counting his money, then passed off. Chico took no time communicating with Keem and the order was delivered. "Alright Popi, stay black and I'll see you tomorrow."

Sleepy almost got hit by Cherie, as she pulled into a parking spot. Chico gave Cherie his undivided attention, as she exited the car. Her figure in business attire made his imagination run wild. Chico adjusted himself, as he watched her saunter home.

"Chico!" Chip barked in an alarming tone, as he exited the vehicle.

"Qué?" Chico quickly looked away.

"Jason, I hope you not drawing my girl," Chip said, as he approached Jason and Shiz.

"Naw, I'm doing my mom's budget," Jason said, with an uncomfortable smile.

"Why are you lying. It's in the momma's boy manual, to give momma the world, without question. How can you budget love?"

"Ok, I'm drawing," Jason admitted.

"That's what's up. It's a lot of cons on death row, who wish they picked up a pencil, instead of a pistol."

Shiz added his two cents, "I'm sure a lot of DOA's, who would feel the same way."

Chip put his handout. "Let me see your artwork."

"I usually don't show my work, but...." Jason tentatively handed over his pad.

Chip's eyes exploded. Once the shock effect departed, his eyes ram sacked the picture, trying to consume every detail. "This picture is off the meat rack; the details are lifelike. The devil's hand, pulling the women's ankle down, is scary good. I don't blame the devil for wanting a piece of her, that's a bad jawn."

"Jason, take that picture from fresh out, before he fresh squeeze on it," Shiz joked.

"Shut up," Chip told Shiz.

"Do you really think I'm a good artist?" Jason inquired.

"Yea." Chip paused to critique Jason's artwork. "Just change a few features in her face. You don't want the world to think you practicing incest. Do you have more artwork?"

"I don't have many sketches, but I have lots of paintings and sculptures," Jason answered.

"Is that why you don't let us in your room? I thought it was because you had a shrine dedicated to your momma or hoagies or something," said Shiz.

"Are you interested in selling your art?" Chip inquired.

"Is elastic waist pants a fat man's best friend?" Jason replied.

"I'll take that as a yes. Let me get a couple art pieces and I'll see if my boy from prison can move them."

Jason folded his arms. "What kind of jailhouse connect is this?"

"My man, use to do B&E's around Montgomery County before getting booked. He had connections who moved his artwork back in the day, I can see if those pipelines are still open. But it's up to you."

Jason shrugged his shoulders, "What do I have to lose."

Chip returned Jason's sketch pad. "Alright, I will grab your artwork after I get a water ice."

"I will be ready." Jason began speed walking, then took off like Michael Johnson at the Olympics. "Momma we gonna be rich!"

Chip chuckled, while Shiz walked around his stand to greet Chip. "What up, my brother." Shiz shook Chips hand, then pulled him in for an embrace. Shiz began frisking Chip with his free hand. Chip pushed Shiz away. "What's wrong fam, no love today?"

Chip was disturbed. "You were rubbing my back."

"Naw bro, your imagination just running gay," Shiz remarked sarcastically.

"Whatever Shiz, let me get a lemon and mango water ice and a bag of popcorn." Chip paid Sheena two dollars.

Shiz passed the bag of popcorn, while his assistant completed the water ice. Once the water ice was prepared, Shiz took it from his assistant, and proceeded to approach Chip. Shiz stumbled and launched the water ice on Chip's fresh white t-shirt. Frantically Chip brushed off the water ice.

"My bad, take off your shirt, and I'll make you another jawn."

"Why do I need to take off my shirt?"

"I don't want you to catch a cold."

"Shiz, it's damn near 90 degrees out here."

"I thought, with you being fresh out, you would be happy to show off your jailhouse tats."

Shiz's assistant prepared another water ice. "I don't have tattoos." Chip snatched the water ice from Sheena before Shiz could reach for it.

"Alright Chip, come again." Shiz waved in Chips direction.

After Chip crossed the street, Shiz said to himself, "I can't believe his rat ass is fucking my girl." Then he flopped down on a white lawn chair.

CHAPTER NINE

"I hope we're not too late." Jason said to himself, as his silver Marauder looked like a bullet, gunning it down 11th Street.

"If you weren't having an eating contest against yourself, we could have been copped upped," Shiz replied.

"You had seconds too." Jason replied and seconds later a grin appeared on his face.

"What are you smiling about, this isn't a Halal food run."

"I'm cheesing, because we're going to make a killing today," Jason foreseen.

"You ain't never lie. It's the first of the month and our work is Mexican labor cheap."

"Our dope is community service cheap," Jason countered.

Shiz rubbed his earlobe, while his eyes searched for nothing in particular. "You know, I'm still not cool with Chip smashing my chick, but he is off my hit list for his good deeds on Warnock Street. Chip is like the ex-con version of Yoda."

Jason bust out laughing. "Today is going to be a great day, if I'm laughing at your corny jokes."

"I should be charging you for these jokes. I'm the funniest bull in the city when Kevin Hart out of town." Shiz got choked up in the seat belt, after Jason slammed on the brakes at a stop sign. "Real rap, you need to slow this mother fucker down, you know I don't have Obama Care and you don't have Allstate."

"Play your position, passenger without a license." Jason snapped back.

"I got whip game though." Shiz imitated a left turn.

"We've been closer than Tia and Tamera our whole life and I have never seen you in a driver seat."

"What about on Grand Theft Auto or Need for Speed. Those cops can't see me." Shiz patted his chest.

"Why can't you ever keep it one hundred?" Jason asked.

"What are you talking about Hefty Man, my word is always bond?"

"You the type of bull, who would try to lie his way out of an interrogation room."

"As you should," Shiz said, with a hand extended.

"I plead the fifth." Jason left Shiz hanging.

Jason turned right on Lehigh Avenue. The corner of Germantown and Lehigh was crawling with everyone and their mother trying to purchase pills. Jason parked close to the action and the two-man crew made their way towards the wholesale drug trade.

"Damn, there's a news van out here." Jason popped up his collar, hoping it would hide his identity.

"Yea, but they're not reporting shit, look." Shiz pointed towards a man and a woman, in business attire, waiting to be served. "Jason go ask them how they feel about the war on drugs."

"I'm on it." Jason rolled down his collar and strolled towards the interviewee. In a confident manner, Jason approach the newsman, with his hand extended like a microphone. "My brother, how do you feel about the war on drugs in North Philly?"

The anchorman checked his surroundings. "Anybody recording this?"

Jason looked suspiciously at the reporter, then responded, "Naw."

Instantly, the anchorman's shoulders relaxed, arms folded, and head cocked to the side. "Real talk, I sold mushrooms to pay for my Penn State education and now I take Percocets to turn me into Superman. Those perks, give me the strength to smile in the face of smokers, with bad breath and deodorant free armpits. Excuse me my brother while I handle my business." The reporter turned back towards the action and yelled, "Who got those perks!"

Shiz decided to try his luck with the female news reporter, who was standing near the news van. "A cutie, you don't smoke tree, do you?"

Shiz gained her undivided attention. "I blow, what'cha got?"

"I got the sweetest cheeba baby. How much are you looking for?"

She placed her hand on her hips. "First, let me see what you working with," she demanded.

Shiz looked over both shoulders, then pulled out a twenty sack of AK-47 and passed it off. She pressed the dub sack against her nostrils and inhaled. The newswoman closed her eyes and moaned.

"Let me get forty and your number. I'll holla back, if it smokes proper," she informed Shiz.

They quickly made the transaction and Shiz gave her his number.

"Don't hesitate to call me, if you want to smoke, fuck, and chill. I meant, smoke and chill." Shiz smirked.

"I'm not about that life. I have a man."

"Your man can't smoke you out like I can," Shiz said with pride.

The reporter gave Shiz the, 'nigga please' look. "My man is negotiating a contract worth forty mill. Smoke that, dope boy."

"Your man looking forward to forty million and you only copping two dub sacks?" Shiz responded with sarcasm.

"Don't worry, I'll hit you up, if your weed smoke proper."

"Real rap, I know I'm not in your man's league, but let me palm your butt and I'll toss you a bag."

She laughed hard. "You shot out. Boy bye." She turned quickly, slapping Shiz with her long ponytail. The anchorwoman approached her co-worker. "I got some smoke, did you get the perks?"

"I got some perks and blues. Let's get shit face and make up a story," he replied, then the news crew got into the news van and raced from the curb.

Jason was talking business with his connect, when Shiz spotted him. Shiz crept up and eased dropped on their conversation.

"Big boy, these Xanies go for a dollar-twenty a pill," said the older man, leaning on a cane.

Jason brows became ruffled. "Old head, my price is a dollar a jawn, not a penny more."

"Alright, you can get them for a dollar a jawn, but let me hold twenty dollars?"

"For what?" Jason asked as if he was considering lending the money.

"Young bull, I'm hot right now and I'll hit you with forty dollars when I get back from Atlantic City."

"Old head, you're not going to hit me with a sob story, how the casino hustled you for my cash. Anyway, here goes my money, now hand me my work." Jason slammed the money into his supplier's hand. Jason was handed a brown bag full of pill bottles.

The old man tapped his cane against the ground. "You a cheap mother fucker."

"Old head, I just tossed you two large, I should be asking you to hold something."

"Just for that, I'm not going to look out when I hit it big in AC."

"You can keep your pipe dreams and I will keep my cash." Jason turned to Shiz. "Let's rout."

As they made their way towards Jason's car, Shiz decided to give Jason the low down. "Can you believe, homegirl wouldn't let me palm her ass for a bag of bud. She was actin like she was too good or something, because her man got that bag."

"She wasn't too good to cop up, now pay up." Jason put his handout.

"Chill, payday collector, I know we are partners," Shiz retorted.

"Speaking of partners, do you think Chico back on the block yet?" Jason asked, as he opened the car door.

CHAPTER TEN

A green Toyota Corolla taxi, parallel parked between an unmarked Tahoe and Lexus 420, on the corner of Kensington and G Street, in the Badlands' section of North Philly. Chico exited the vehicle and kicked a carryout container out of his way.

"Ready rock, ready rock," was marketed in Chico's direction by a Puerto Rican kid from the corner of Kensington Avenue.

Chico paid the young bull no mind and ducked his head back into the taxi. "You know the deal Noir."

"My friend, take your time," Noir replied calmly, in his thick Sierra Leonean accent.

"Oh yea, Rell said he gonna bless you, for rolling with me on that move."

Noir slowly winked at Chico. "I had a ball making them suffer."

Chico became uncomfortable after hearing Noir's comment. "People talk that gangster shit, that they will cut your balls off and hand them to you; but you actually cut someone's balls off and let him hold them in their mouth." Chico cringed.

"Why do you look uncomfortable? You know I don't play swords with other men. Matter fact, Marlena has a friend for you." Noir smiled. "Be my wingman."

"The last time I was your wingman, my leg was about to be amputated from the lack of blood flow. On that note, I'm good." Chico closed door.

Noir rolled down the passenger window, "You're missing out. The heavier the woman, the heavier the loving. Plus, big girls never go dry."

"That's true, but I'm good." Chico began walking away.

Noir stuck his head out the passenger window, "Ask your cousin, has he ever caught rug burn between the thighs of a voluptuous woman?"

Chico put a thumb in the air and kept it moving. While traveling to Rell's operation, Chico checked his surroundings. No real foot traffic was on the block, but dope boys posted on each corner of the block. Vehicles parked along the curve were head turners. A few luxury cars and SUV's, were parked back to back, in front of boarded up and rundown homes. Three unmarked police vehicles were also parked on the block, but they were also some of Rell's normal speakeasy clientele.

Chico walked up the front steps, then softly knocked on the door. The door was unlocked and slightly opened by Rell's huge doorman. The gatekeeper looked Chico up and down, then moved to the side. A sawed-off shotgun fell to the doorman's side, as Chico entered the house. John Coltrane's saxophone serenaded the atmosphere, as he parted a red beaded entrance. Rell's heaven on earth was covered wall to wall with luxurious red carpet. Fine art paintings decorated the eggshell white walls. Elegant chandeliers showcased man's most alluring vices. Playmates dressed in bras, garter belts, thongs, and hosiery seduced professional men on and off the clock. Men in suits, placed bets on craps and roulette, in the living room of the row home. A group of cops shared a laugh at the bar, in what would've been the living room of a normal row home. Three men were seated at the kitchen table, waiting to be served by a gourmet chef. The smell of cigar smoke drifted from the basement. A tan Cuban vixen, led an older gentleman upstairs, for an afternoon quickie.

A stampede of ravishing ladies sashayed in Chico's direction as he made his way to the dining room. His wet dream faded away, once the playmates recognized it was only Rell's little cousin. As the gorgeous women retreated, Chico spotted the mastermind, cloaked in a red silk robe and matching slippers; assuredly seated on a lavish black leather club chair, adjected from the bar.

"Jesus," Rell joyfully greeted his cousin.

Chico approached his relative and got right to business, "I need two gallons of dust juice."

"Como esta to you too, Warren Buffet," Rell joked.

"You taught me business first and small talk kills," Chico reminded him.

"Yo creado un monstru."

"Why do I have to be a monster? You told me always stick to the script," Chico quoted Rell once more.

"Alright primo, let's get down to business." Rell looked towards the bar and called out, "Blackberry." Rell waved over a 5'11", dark skin diva, sporting a red bodysuit and matching heels. The Jet Beauty of the Week slowly sauntered over to the master of the house. On arrival, she backhanded Rell, straddled his lap, then kissed him furiously.

Chico silently looked on, until Rell attempted to unzip her bodysuit. "Yo, I'm not watching you fuck again."

Rell leered at his dominatrix goddess. "Tonight, we are putting those paddles and handcuffs to work."

"Rell, business first." Chico reminded him once again.

Chico broke Rell's lustful gaze, "Chica, conseguir dos galones de agua para mi familia." Rell order the Columbian beauty.

"Si Popi," she responded, then switched off.

Rell bit on his thumb, "Primo, do you see how loose that brown booty is?" Chico didn't respond. Rell turned his attention back to his cousin. "It's not good to be all business primo. Even God rested on the seventh day." Once again, Chico didn't respond.

Blackberry returned with a grocery bag and handed it to Chico. "Gracias' bonita." Rell snapped his finger and pointed towards the bar. With no rap, she returned to her post. Chico put down the bag, removed the payment from his back pocket, and paid his supplier.

The money was stuffed into Rell's robe pocket, then he examined his cousin. "Primo, you starting to accumulate a lot of fedia, it's time for you to start thinking about starting a business."

"Like this tax-free brothel?" Chico joked.

"You stupid, I'm taxing the shit out of these hoes." Rell Chuckled, then continued, "All jokes aside, you need a business like my car detail shop on Front Street or my corner store on Allegheny Ave."

"Why do I need a business, when my operation is doing great?"

"Just like every other nigga that run in and out of those Correctional Facilities, you're not thinking ahead."

Chico rolled his eyes. "What's the problem?"

"If Johnny Law came knocking today, how would you explain, the thousands of dollars under your pissy mattress?" Rell quizzed his unprepared cousin.

Chico rubbed his chin. "Alright Rell, school me."

"Most people think hard about how to get in the dope game, while the five percent of the population, who run the world, know the truth about drug money."

"What's the truth?"

"The truth is, drug money ain't worth their time, if they can't launder it." Rell paused to collect his thoughts. "If you want to buy a luxury car or house, without your name popping up on the FBI's radar, you better have tax returns, explaining your earthly endeavors," warned Rell.

Chico nodded his head. "I can dig that."

"Well, it gets deeper Primo. Money to most people only represents a key to obtaining luxury goods or covering their basic needs. But to the few who know the secret to wealth, consider their dollars as workers, soldiers or slaves. They put their dollars into investments and now those dollars live to make them more dollars. What I'm getting at, is the real game is not how to get into the dope game, it's how to get out of the game, when you're ready to quit, with money still coming in, so you don't have to go back to those unsafe streets. At my level of the game, money flows to me from different revenue streams and to be honest, you're a slave to my drug trade enterprise." Rell tapped Chico's bankroll in his pocket.

"Rell, you're being really disrespectful right now," Chico replied angrily.

Rell laughed. "Hear me out primo. You're hustling to re-up and I'm the man with the work. Right?"

"That's true."

"Don't feel bad, you have slaves too. People work nine to five's, rob, steal, sell drugs, operate businesses, and anything else the mind can conceive to buy from you. The difference between you and I, is my money is working hard to build me a fantastic future and your money is going to work to keep you at work. Yi mean?"

"I can dig that, thanks for pulling my card." Chico gave Rell a handshake, then embraced for a hug.

"No problem Primo. Now, go be a good worker and come back soon." Rell smiled, awaiting Chico's response. Rell's sarcasm brought an enlightened smile upon Chico's face and he was on his way.

<u>CHAPTER ELEVEN</u>

There wasn't a customer insight, as Noir returned Chico to Warnock Street. Chico checked his surroundings, as Noir parked in front of Jason's house. Chico turned to Noir and extended his right hand, "Good looking Noir, I'll hit you up next week."

Noir shook his hand, but he wasn't ready to part. "Do me a favor and take one for the team? I need you to be my wingman."

"Noir, I'm not about that widebody life," Chico declined.

"I know your hefty friend, from fruits of Islam, is pressed on his mom, but what about your starving friend?"

"That's not gonna fly. His girl could headline the Asian version of Jet Beauty of the Week. How about you run a train on both jawns. You said, the bigger the girl, the bigger the loving."

Noir scratched his chin. "It would be the ultimate sandwich. Chicken wings and weed would have them open, like hood rats on ball players." Noir paused, then continued, "You should do me this favor though, I castrated a man for you."

"You shouldn't tell people you took that one for the team," Chico recommended.

Before Noir could respond, Shiz came yelling in their direction. "Yo Noir, let me holla at you playboy." Shiz jogged to the driver side of the vehicle and looked at Chico. "Popi, take a walk, grown folks are talking."

Chico exited the car, proceeded to the trunk and removed the grocery bag full of dust juice.

Shiz waited till Chico was on his way, to converse with Noir, "Where's your cousin at, I'm looking for those Booty Talk flicks." Shiz attempted to shake Noir's hand.

"You're crazy, if you think I'm shaking your hand, after asking me for porn." Noir examined Shiz's hand, gave him a head nod, and bounced.

Shiz examined his right hand, sniffed his fingernails, shrugged, then made his way back to Jason's house. As Shiz entered the house, he spotted Jason on the edge of his couch watching the Food Network. Shiz sat on a love seat to the right of Jason. "Hey gluttony of the eyes, Chico is back. Didn't you say we on the block as soon as Chico came back?" Jason ignored Shiz's comment.

Once a commercial came on, Jason hesitantly departed the couch, to grab the left over work from last night. Chico entered the house, as Jason ascended the stairs.

Shiz approached Chico and asked, "Is it odd that Jason watches Food Network all day, but we never seen him cook?"

"I never thought about it, but that is pretty weird," Chico agreed.

"He even creating paintings of whole meals, with the Hawaiian Rolls on the side. Food fetish is written all over bull," Shiz believed.

"Stop hating, because he got dreams of pigging out. You need to buy one of his paintings, so you can get over your anorexia."

"Girls dig this Slim Jim frame." Shiz imitated poses from J.J. from Good Times.

"It must hurt banging pelvis to pelvis with your bony girl. That's why I don't smash skinny jawns."

"You not smashing shit, because Abuela only leaves the house to pay tithes and grocery shop."

Chico and Shiz turn towards the stairs, as Jason rumbled down, with a brown lunch bag in hand.

"Boys be safe," Jason mom screamed from the top of the stairs.

"Yes, ma'am," The crew song in unison.

WARNOCK UNCUT

Jason passed the brown bag to Chico and it disappeared into his underwear before exiting the house. Chico immediately stashed the inventory, then went to recruit Keem. A half-hour later, Jason's eyes were restless, due to non-stop foot traffic. Jason noticed, each person who purchased from Chico, had a water ice in hand. Seeing Shiz's talent bring joy to the masses, made Jason's desire to become a famous artist intensify.

By the time the second break approached, Keem had wiggled his finger under his nose twelve times, signaling Jason to replenish the stash. Jason, Shiz, and Chico could barely stay seated during their break.

"Dawg, my dick been Viagra hard, thinking about the money I'm collecting off this EBT app," Shiz stated. Jason and Chico stepped back from their energized companion.

"Jason, remember that three hundred and twenty-five dollars of that EBT money, belongs to the dope game," Chico recapped.

"This is crazy, we're making food stamp money. Shiz, that water ice stand was the smartest idea you ever conceived," Jason admitted.

"I'm getting props for my genius. And to think, this moment came from me chasing my dreams."

Shiz's comment made Jason look away. After watching the 'Secret' DVD, he created a vision board, with images and words, of the heights he desired to reach. Jason envisioned having a statue created in his image, because of his great works, just like Thomas Eakins.

Chico tapped Jason, snapping him out of his dream like state. "How did we become friends with such a cornball?"

"I'm not a cornball, I'm a cheeseball. Yi mean?" Shiz tapped his pockets.

Chico was about to put in an objection, but Cherie and Chip pulling up, gained his undivided attention. The driver side door swung open and the beautiful Cherie emerged in business attire.

"Muy guopa," Slipped from Chico's lips.

"Telemundo, I don't know what you just said, but I'm sure we're on the same page," Shiz responded.

Cherie waited until Chip exited the car, then she approached him, "From drug lord to mentor, can you be any sexier?" She kissed him softly, then switched off. After watching his lady walk away, he ventured towards Warnock Crew, sporting an ear to ear smile.

"What's good OG, how's our lady doing?" Shiz asked Chip, as soon as his foot landed on Jason's property.

Chip shook his head, but his smile remained. "You know the Bible states, 'Even a fool is considered wise when he keeps silent.'"

"You clowning me with verses from the Bible? Oh, that's got to be against a commandment, sin, or something." Shiz believed.

"You're lucky, God loves fools and babies," Chip countered, then turned his attention to the whole crew. "I got good news."

"Is Trump giving out reparations in the form of free admission to all strip clubs, during black history month." Shiz guessed.

"Do you think before you speak?" asked Jason.

"Think my brother." Shiz tapped his temple, then continued, "When you have a gifted mind like mine, it would be stupid to do that."

"Allah, help this child." Chip massaged his temple.

"I thought you were Christian?" Jason asked Chip.

Chip flung his arms in the air. "Does it matter...."

Before Chip could continue, Chico added his two cents, "It kind of does matter, Abuela cooks everything with pork."

"Enough!" Chip yelled.

"Oh, angry black man," Chico said under his breath.

"The reason I was happy, before encountering Shiz." He paused to show his irritation. Then he focused on the man of the hour. "Jason is four thousand dollars richer."

"What?" all the boys said in unison.

"One of Jason's statues sold for four thousand dollars. We had a couple offers for your other art pieces, but experts believe you can earn more by waiting. Congratulations." Chip pulled out a check from his back pocket and passed it to the sculptor.

Jason passed the check to Chico and pulled Chip in for a bear hug. Chip's feet dangled like a child in its mother's arms. Jason swung him back and forth like a rag doll. "The law of attraction really works."

"Alright Goliath, put me down."

Jason followed Chip's order and gave his appreciation, "You made my day Chip, thank you."

"That's a first. He never said that before, without a calorie being gained," said Shiz.

"Your ignorance isn't going to kill my joy today," Jason said to Shiz, then took his check from Chico. After one glance, he took off into the house. "Momma, we are hitting IHOP in the morning. I'm a celebrity."

"Prime example of fat people, making it bigger." Shiz shook his head.

"Shut up," Chip and Chico responded.

CHAPTER TWELVE

On a baking hot summer afternoon, the crew regrouped in front of Jason's house, for their second break. Everyone but Jason was devouring their sandwiches and guzzling water.

Chico noticed Jason not eating and spoke up, "Picasso, you not hungry?"

"Don't you mean Chubby Devinci?" Shiz clowned.

"Chubby Devinci," Jason pondered aloud. "I like it, I'm getting husky off art money."

"Naw, you husky off seconds and thirds." Shiz joked.

"Ock, my last check was 10k. Eat that, icy boy." Jason gave Shiz the people eyebrow.

"Dawg, you actin like you the only one eating out here. My last EBT check was 5k." Shiz returned Jason's people eyebrow.

"One of those K's belong to the dope game," Chico set the record straight.

Shiz flung his arms in the air. "Come on Knee High, you could have pulled my card after me and Jason got done talking shit."

"I'm just making sure you don't come at us later saying, 'I caught the munchies at Ruth's Chris' or 'we trying to burn you because you high'," Chico explained.

"Pigmy Perez, Ruth's Chris only happened once and these hands not busting no suds." Shiz looked at his partners and asked, "Any who, do anyone want a water ice?"

"Let me get a passion fruit and you should have the same. Maybe, it'll give you the passion, to cash a 10k check," Jason suggested.

"Whatever Elastic Clothes Man." Shiz turned to Chico, "Do you want anything?"

"Naw, I need both hands free."

Shiz nodded positively at Chico's response. "Just making sure you're focused."

Chico steered into Shiz's slightly bloodshot eyes. "Are you focused? I can tell you've been getting lit."

"My bad, some customers sparked a blunt next to the stand and I got weaker than Pookie in the Carter."

"You look like Pookie, with those dusty ass lips," Chico replied, and Jason began rolling.

Shiz swiped his tongue back and forth on his lips, like a windshield wiper, then responded, "You lucky I gotta get this money. All I dream of is cracking jokes on the heightly challenged and you look like a dream come true."

"Get back to work," ordered Jason.

As Shiz walked away, he began mouthing off, "I'm the boss of this cartel. Scooby Doo doesn't bark orders to Shaggy. So, find a Scooby Snack or solve the mystery of that extra chin appearing beneath your chin."

Chico conversed with Keem, to ensure everything was ready to go. Shiz unlocked his freezer box, while cracking jokes on his assistant. Jason placed a newspaper on his lap, then scoped out his environment. Twenty minutes later, transactions were being made by Chico and Shiz. Both merchants had a respectable line awaiting service. The adults were acting pettier than the children in Shiz's operation. One woman asked to do rock, paper, scissor to gain a better spot in line. Two grown men had to be sent to the back of the line, for cutting in front of some kids.

Shiz spotted a white Charger, speeding in his direction. "Adios amigos," Shiz screamed out in Chico's direction.

Chico walked away from a customer, not caring about her response. Instead of the police pulling in front of Chico's operation, they stopped in front of Shiz's water ice stand. With no hesitation, Shiz nudged his assistant to take a walk. The same cops, who were chased off by gunfire, emerged from the Charger.

"Shit," Shiz mumbled under his breath, as both cops made their way to the front of the line.

"You cursed and I'm telling my mom." A little girl, at the front of the line, spoke up.

"Don't act holier than thou, I know you and your momma watch Love and Hip Hop together." Shiz responded to the minor and she looked away.

Officer Kemp, bumped into the tattle tale, without an apology given. "Really?" The little girl rolled her eyes, then continued. "Your parents didn't teach you no manners."

"Be quiet Annie, before you get lost in the system," Kemp responded, then looked up and down the line. "Matter of fact, the water ice stand is closed, everyone take a walk."

An older man did the shoulder bounce as he walked away. "You don't have to tell me twice. My pockets funkier than Snoop's crib."

The little girl stood her ground and flashed her EBT card. "I'm a paying customer and we're not slaves any longer, Uncle Tom."

Officer Kemp snatched her card and flung it in the street. "If you don't want me to cut up your livelihood, you better be moving along." The law enforcer made scissor fingers.

The little girl retrieved the card and walked off, but her lips continued to flap, "My momma would piece you up, talking about messing with our livelihood. You need to ease up on your livelihood, small uniform man."

Shiz rolled his eyes, "I hope y'all here to get served, because my vending license is good," Shiz said confidently.

The white officer, began poking Shiz as he spoke, "We didn't ask you that. You speak, when spoken too, boy."

"This is a shakedown." Officer Kemp cleared his throat, then continued, "I mean protection, my brother."

"Pig, we are not brothers, you ugly as shit. You so ugly, my momma wouldn't claim you, on a tax return."

"Twenty percent of your profits is ours from now on," Kemp informed Shiz.

"Twenty percent for what? My hood pass is good around here. Maybe I should be offering you protection. Didn't you two get shot at the last time you popped up on my block?" Shiz smirked.

"Look here boy." The white cop got in Shiz's face. "This is a dictatorship and you're a peasant on our land."

"Suck me badge." Shiz grinned at his extorters, while fondling his genitals. The white officer, quickly seized Shiz by the back of his neck and slammed his slim frame down on a freezer box.

Chico peeped game from behind a car, then yelled in Jason's direction. "Yo Jason, we have a big problem." Then Chico sprinted towards Shiz. "Get off my boy."

The white cop released Shiz and approached Chico. "Or what runt?"

"Or I'll report you." Chico examined his badge. "Officer Dunwrong."

"What's the deal Chico?" Jason inquired half winded.

Shiz quickly spoke up "These pussies are trying to extort..."

Before Shiz could continue his spill, a gut check from the white officer, sent Shiz to his knees.

Jason saw red and eagerly approached to avenge his friend. Jason's energy took a diabetic coma, as Kemp raised his peacemaker and in his direction. Kemp, scanned Warnock Crew, as if he was trying to figure something out, then it hit him, "Y'all under arrest."

"For what?" Chico sounded hysterical. "We didn't do shit. Y'all the criminals,"

"Wrong, you hooligans are resisting our Stop and Frisk investigation," Kemp responded.

"Put your hands on the icebox or y'all won't be making it to trial like Trayvon Martin," ordered Officer Dunwrong.

Warnock Crew, placed their hands on the ice box, then officer Dunwrong read them their lack of rights. They were frisked, cuffed, and shoved in the back of the Charger. Threw the tight streets of Philly, the patrol vehicle raced to the 18th Precinct, with cherry's flaring and siren roaring. When they arrived at the precinct, Jason exited the squad car first, then Shiz, followed by Chico.

"Do y'all see how husky my man is?" Shiz did a double head nod towards Jason. "You know he paddy wagon material."

Chico was enraged. "We are getting arrested and you worried about the comfort of your ride. There is no denying it, you're a full-blown retard."

"You know I'm sensitive about my learning speed." With hands cuffed behind their backs, Chico and Shiz, furiously bumped against each other. After the officers stopped laughing, they separated them.

Chico spoke up first, "My bad for spazzing on you. If we weren't cuffed, we could bro hug it out."

"I could use a bro hug and a blunt right now."

"Ralph Tresvant and Chico DeBarge, keep it moving; this ain't the sensitivity hour." Officer Kemp, shoved the two friends into the 18th Precinct, to begin running their credentials through the mud.

<u>CHAPTER THIRTEEN</u>

Jason and Shiz, leaned on the locked up freezer boxes, contemplating the future of their businesses on Warnock Street. Abruptly, Abuela's front door flew open and Chico darted out hugging a suitcase. Abuela launched a bookbag at Chico, that slammed into the small of his back. The impact sent Chico crashing to the concrete.

"Diablo licencia!" Abuela yelled, then slammed the door.

Shiz broke the silence, "I knew Abuela was going to put a foot in his ass, but I didn't think he would get evicted."

"Let's find out what's the verdict." Jason began walking and Shiz followed.

"You good Popi?" Jason asked as he approached.

"I couldn't get the door unlocked fast enough," Chico sounded delusional.

"She should get a medal for her technique and distance," Shiz injected.

While picking up Chico's backpack, Jason asked, "Did you get evicted?"

"She's not planning a lawn sale."

"Didn't you tell her, you were protecting Shiz?" asked Jason.

"That isn't why she's buggin. She trippin, because I didn't try to escape and start a revolución'."

Shiz chuckled, then asked, "Who does she think you are, Fidel Castro?"

"She knows, you only got hit with resisting arrest, right?" asked Jason.

"She told me, 'Only puta's get charged with resisting arrest."

Shiz exhaled. "That lady hard as nails."

"But that's not why I got evicted," Chico said, while rubbing his back.

Jason was confused. "Then, why did you get the boot?"

"Abuela told me to read the Book of Exodus, then I got kicked out."

"What?" Jason and Shiz looked dumbfounded.

"She asked me, 'What did I learn from the story of Moses?' I told her, 'Pharaoh was an idiot for not killing Moses, when he first returned on that, 'Let my people go' campaign'."

"Are you stupid? Old people don't play that questioning the Bible shit." Shiz said.

"Fuck that, we should do to those cops, what Pharaoh should have done to Moses; smoked him and got right back to the money," Chico said with vengeance.

Shiz looked away and said, "This nigga trippin."

Jason placed a hand on Chico's shoulder. "Popi fall back, these cops are drawlin already. And I know you don't want to get Stopped and Frisked every day; because that'll be the outcome of another fallen cop in Philly."

"Well, what are we gonna do?" Chico asked Jason.

Jason thought about it for a second, then said, "We're not broke, maybe it's time to change hustles."

"I hear you, but my resume only has one occupation. My cover letter will be titled, 'Dope Boy Extraordinaire'." Chico motioned his hands, like the title was in bright lights.

"Naw, Jason might be on to something." Shiz nodded, then continued, "We should sell sex toys at bachelorette parties."

"Do you see how young Chico look? He would make women feel like pedophiles."

Shiz sucked his teeth and spoke his mind, "Some women are into that."

"Stupid, I don't think my grandma would like my picture in the back of the Daily News, holding a rubber dick."

"Maybe a sex toy would loosen her up," said Shiz.

Chico attempted to steal Shiz, but Jason held him back. "Sex toys and Abuela is a dead convo, alright." Chico demeanor screamed, 'don't get fucked up'.

"Well, that was my good idea," stated Shiz.

Jason chuckled and asked, "What was your bad idea?"

"Starting a sex hotline."

"If Abuela recognized my voice, on one of those midnight infomercials, she would drop dead. Shiz, sex and business is dead. Alright?"

"Let me think. Ummmm...." Shiz placed his index finger over his lips.

Jason looked and raised his hands towards the heavens. "Please God, let him think."

Instantly, an idea came to Shiz, "I got the water ice game on smash, how about we start a water ice business like Rita's?"

"That sounds good, but it's almost fall. Plus, you know my artwork goes for five stacks or better. How about we open an art gallery?" countered Jason.

"Your art isn't going to sell every day, but my water ice sells all day and night, like crack on Diamond Street."

"Your money good in spring and summer, but like I said, the hulk will be out soon," disputed Jason.

Jason and Shiz, stood belly to ribs, going idea for idea. Shiz came back with, "We can flip hot chocolate and soft pretzels when it's hulking."

"Bro, I'm not trying to be sniffling in the cold, selling dollar hot chocolates."

Chico forced his way in-between the think tank. "I got it. How about an Art Gallery, that serves water ice?"

They looked at each other in silence, feeling out the idea. Chico began to slowly nod his head, the other two did the same and slowly stepped back.

"Scarface that is a thurl idea, but if any girls ask, I came up with it," Shiz alleged.

"If anyone ask why you work there, we'll tell them, we're receiving the special needs tax break." Jason laughed at Chico's wit.

"Whatever. What are we going to call our business?" Shiz paused, then continued. "How about 'Shiz's Place'?"

"You really wear your narcissism on your sleeve," Jason thought.

"Alright, forget about Shiz's Place. How about Three the Hard Way or The G Spot."

Chico asked Shiz, "What's up with all the sexual suggestions?"

"Kim been on the rag for about a week. I'm ready to run a red light, yi mean?"

"I wish I didn't, yi mean" Chico responded.

"Whatever." Shiz rolled his eyes, then continued, "These ideas started on Warnock Street, so let's call it Warnock Art Gallery." Everyone nodded in agreement.

Chico followed up, "We're gonna need a good lawyer to handle the paperwork and my cousin has a great one that works for weed."

Shiz asked Chico, "What can a stoned lawyer do for us?"

"Homeboy, has cleaned up more dirty money, than the Kennedy family after prohibition."

"Sold," Shiz responded.

"Me too," Jason stated while watching Noir park.

Shiz was the first one to cut into Noir, as he exited the car. "A Noir, I need to holla at your cousin?"

"What's wrong now?" Noir questioned, while taking the bookbag from Jason.

"The flick he sold me, had the wrong disk in the case."

"A flick is a flick, right?" Noir asked, while grabbing Chico's suitcase.

"That jawn, had animals beating cheeks, and Old McDonald style porn isn't my twist."

"Sorry about your experience, but he's on State Road," Noir replied, as he closed the trunk.

"That man gets locked up more than DMX," Shiz stated.

"He got caught with heroin, DVD's, and Jordan's. It's all good though, he'll be home soon."

"Does he have Diplomatic immunity or friends in the CIA?" questioned Jason.

Noir shrugged, "Nope, we keep Grant Freeman on retainer."

"That's the lawyer we're going to use," Chico informed his squad, as he entered the passenger side of the vehicle.

"Where are you headed? I hope not to meet up with those cops," Jason prayed.

Chico avoided eye contact with Jason, "Naw, they off the hook. Noir taking me to a room & board, off 22nd and Lippincott."

"Word? Can I bring Kim through, when my mom gets back?" Shiz eagerly asked Chico.

"Drive," Chico ordered Noir and they were on their way.

CHAPTER FOURTEEN

From the heavens above, Downtown Philadelphia looked like an ant farm, with cars and foot traffic struggling to maneuver through these tunnels we call streets. On the corner of Broad and Chestnut, the Warnock three emerged from the subway station and ventured west on Chestnut Street. Jason and Chico, had to yank Shiz from cracking on every fine woman he encountered, on their journey to 16th Street.

As they approached the entrance of the skyscraper, Shiz amplified his stride.   "Let's go lackeys." Hostilely, Shiz shoved opened the glass door and it shattered against a marble wall. Every patron in the lobby stopped to observe the fiasco. Shiz shrugged off the calamity and kept it moving; while Jason and Chico, bowed their head in shame, as they followed their overzealous companion.

Shiz approached the elevator operator with a head nod, "What up chief? We're going up, way up, yi mean?"

"No sir, I do not understand? What level do you wish to ascend too?" The elevator operator sounded like Jeffery from Fresh Prince.

"You're working in Philly and you don't understand 'yi mean'. Someone needs to work on your people skills. Now repeat after me, Yiiii...."

Jason swooped in to cover Shiz's mouth, then addressed the elevator operator, "We're headed to the 12th floor, sir."

The elevator operator pressed twelve on the keypad and the elevator doors split. Jason shoved his slim friend into the confined space, then Jason and Chico entered the elevator. Chico and Jason smiled like angels, until the doors closed.

Chico bellowed, "Are you fucking loco? We're around white folks. If you're not Richard Pryor, Tracy Morgan, or Samuel L Jackson, white people don't want to see a crazy black man in person."

Shiz folded his arms. "I can tell type of slaves y'all would have been. And the word house comes to mind."

"You're at a ten Shiz and we need you at a one." Jason motioned with his hands.

"It's y'all fault." Shiz pointed at his companions, then continued, "Who wanted me sober for this meeting? Y'all know, I'm like a kid in a toy store without my meds."

'Bing', the elevator doors parted, and Shiz sped out. "The boss leads the pack."

"Get'cha black ass back here." Jason gripped Shiz by the neck and slung him to the back of the group.

"True, true, true, bodyguards go first," Shiz stated while unraveling his collar.

"Naw, we want to come off as competent. So Shiz, only speak when spoken too," Jason ordered.

"Who do you think you talking to Lassie? Remember, you only bark when I'm in trouble."

"Please Shiz, act like you have a little common sense when we get in here," Chico pleaded with holy hands.

"Little bit, I'm as cool as a fan."

Jason began walking, then paused to examine Shiz, closed his eyes, exhaled, then turned to open the door that read, 'Law Office of Grant Freeman'. One by one, the crew entered the office. A secretary, who was seated behind her desk, stood to greet the boys.

"God damn, that's a bad jawn," rushed from Shiz's pie hole.

Jason hurled his arms in the air, then turned to address his partner, "What did we just discuss?"

"Jason, do you see those puppies busting out the top of her blouse? Those knockers look like two Milk Duds, fresh out the pack, and I know you love Milk Duds."

Jason turned to examine the chocolate beauty. The secretary had curves that could make an S jealous or make a momma's boy forget home. Jason presented a goofy smile in her direction, "I would love for that chocolate to melt in my mouth," he responded in a dream like trance. Abruptly, Jason snapped out of his trance and spazzed on Shiz, "Don't use my weakness to blow off your ignorance."

Chico shhh'd, Jason and Shiz, as the 5'11 bombshell approached. "How are you gentlemen doing today?"

Shiz made his move, "You know they say, 'the darker the berry, the sweeter the juice', right."

"I've heard that a time or two." Her full lips parted and presented a flawless smile.

"Well, you look sweet enough to cause instant diabetes." Shiz slowly looked her up and down.

Her deep dimples and blushing cheeks enhanced her allure. "That was original and cute," she responded.

"So, do you have a Trans Pass? I would love to give you the business. I mean show you my business." Chico connected a jab to Shiz's arm, causing Shiz clinched his teeth to hold back the pain.

"Sorry ma'am, he has Tourette's. We have an appointment with Mr. Freeman," Jason informed her.

"Ok, have a seat. He should be wrapping up his appointment soon."

The crew backed into their seats, without taking an eye off the secretary. "Damn!" Warnock Crew sung in unison, as she returned to her desk. Jason and Chico, looked away quickly after committing their act of folly, while Shiz blatantly kept looking upon her Serena Williams like figure.

She looked over her shoulder and hypothesized, "I guess you all have a case of Tourette's, huh?"

Shiz sprung to his feet. "Fuck what he talking about baby, I don't have Tourette's. You bad ass shit and I would love to be your shadow. Are you trying to pose for Snapchat..." Chico and Jason yanked Shiz into his seat. The secretary giggled at the Three Stooges, as she took her seat.

"You have truly lost your damn mind. Your friends with Kim on every social media platform," Chico informed his thirsty friend.

"Kim who?" Shiz looked at Chico like he was stupid.

The secretary cut in, "I love a straightforward man, but I have a man."

"My bad for coming at you like that," Shiz said sincerely.

"Don't apologize, it just lets me know, I'm still the talk of the town."

Jason gawked at her puppies. "Mmmm, chocolate."

"Did you say something Hun?" Her comment snapped Jason out of his Homer like trance and he shook his head no.

Before the secretary could notify Mr. Freeman, his office door opened, and two men exited. A European man, with a thick Scottish accent, began talking to a Spanish man who wore a neck brace. "Romero, remember no more slip and fall cases. Your name is hot in that industry. Go for car accidents or the bug in the food gimmick."

"Si, Si, mi amigo."

"Romero, you don't have to play that, 'I don't speaka any English bit', with me," Mr. Freeman advised his client.

Romero's dialect transformed into a Harvard Law grad, "I know, but practice makes perfect, comprenda?"

"I understand, just don't bring me any more slip and fall cases, comprenda."

Romero nodded his head and the two men shook hands.

Romero walked towards the exit and Mr. Freeman walked towards his secretary, unaware of his new client's presence. "How are my friends doing?" The lawyer leaned in to motorboat her twin peaks.

Loudly she cleared her throat. "We have clients waiting."

Mr. Freeman giggled, then made a swift about face. "Hey fellas, let's talk in my office."

MICHAEL HIGGINS JR.

The boys complied and Mr. Freeman shook their hands as they entered his office. Wall to wall, Mr. Freeman's office was covered with awards, certificates, degrees, and pictures of him shaking hands with top dogs in Philadelphia. The crew, sat in lavish wooden chairs, adjacent to Mr. Freeman's dark cedar wood desk.

Before their advocate could take a seat, Shiz was on his case, "My man, how did you bag homegirl?"

"As you youths would say." Freeman performed quotation with his fingers, then continued, "That bad jawn was looking for a gig and I needed an assistant, so I hired her. I eased dropped on a conversation and found out that she liked kinky men. So, one day, I acted hammered after lunch and I asked her, 'Have you ever had two in the pink and one in the stink?'. As you can see, my recklessness didn't get me a sexual harassment lawsuit."

Shiz slapped the table. "Y'all white bulls are freaks."

A sly smile was presented by Mr. Freeman. "If you're not freaking out, then sex is just another nut. And you can get that by yourself." Mr. Freeman adjusted his tie, then got down to business, "So, how can I be of service to you?"

Chico spoke up, "We want to start an art gallery, that serves water ice."

"You must be Jesus. Tell Rell I have a business meeting scheduled for Tuesday and I need three Latin ladies by 6pm."

"What's wrong with your phone?" questioned Chico.

"You're here, he's in Badlands, and we don't talk on the phones. And remember, you're getting a friend of the family rate for my valued service," Freeman stated quickly.

"Consider it done."

Mr. Freeman picked up a fancy Fountain pen, removed the cover, then turned to a fresh sheet in his journal. "What is the name of the business?"

"Warnock Art Gallery, yi mean?" Shiz answered with gusto.

"I yi mean," Mr. Freeman answered. "Do you mind if I finish this line, Yi mean?"

Shiz looked puzzled, but proceeded to answer, "Sure."

Mr. Freeman pulled out his center drawer, that exposed some pre-made lines of coke on a mirror. With no shame in his game, he grabbed a pre-rolled dollar bill and went to town. "Hooyah!" Mr. Freeman slapped the desk top, as he came up for air. Once he cleaned off his nostrils, he decided to share the wealth. "This blow could put an elephant on its ass. Y'all want a bump?" The boys slowly turned their heads from east to west.

"So, where were we?" Mr. Freeman's eyes ransacked the room looking for a clue. "Oh yea, the gallery, slash water ice business venture. So, you will need to incorporate under an LLC partnership, so someone like me, won't leave you broker than Detroit. You will

154

also need a license to serve food, a tax id number, and other minor paperwork. I will connect you with my business accountant to reduce your taxes. You will also need insurance to protect your business from whatever comes your way. I will sign you up to SAM, just in case you want to do business with the government one day. I'll create a winning business plan and proposal, so you can get some grant money for your minority owned business. We will need a location near your target market, which I will find via the Small Business Administration. How does everything sound so far?" The crew was speechless, but they nodded in agreement. Mr. Freeman continued to advise, "You will need to set up a business account with a bank or credit union. I prefer credit unions. Now, onto my compensation." The mastermind rubbed his palms together. "It would cost the average Joe over ten thousand dollars for my full service, plus three thousand to keep me on retainer. But you're a friend of the family and I need something you have."

"Fam, we not with that gay shit and Chico underage," Shiz spat out.

Mr. Freeman hysterically laughed. "You are hilarious. I'm not trying to go tip to bum with you guys. Rell tells me that you have some Grade A skunk. Is this true?"

"Hell yea, my bud is the best in the city." Shiz tapped his index finger on the expensive desktop.

"Why does every weed dealer say that?" Freeman questioned.

"I would let you try some, but these squares." Shiz pointed at his companions, then continued, "Made me leave my bud at home."

"I'm sure your smoke is terrific, but the only thing I smoke is cigars. Now my lady on the other hand, gets loose after a good joint. For that purpose, I will need two pounds of skunk." Mr. Freeman put the cap on his pen, at the end of his speech.

"No problem, we will bring it tomorrow," Chico replied.

"Excellent, I will start on the business plan ASAP. Who should I contact, if I have any questions?"

Jason announced, "Chico is our business manager."

Chico's head snapped in Jason's direction. "Real rap?"

"Why not. Shiz and I need to focus on our crafts. You're smart, good with numbers, and a bulldog when it comes to handling business. Do you want the position or not?" Chico leaped out his seat and hugged Jason. "I'll take that as a yes."

Mr. Freeman scratched his head at the sight. "Well Chico, after your done bro hugging, give me your number and we're done for today."

Chico regained his sturdy image and recited his number to Mr. Freeman. The fellas exchanged handshakes, then Mr. Freeman escorted them out of his office.

"Alright Warnock Crew, I will see you tomorrow." He waved goodbye to his new clients, then he approached his lover. "Darling, we're going to Victoria Secret. I can imagine you in some bright red lingerie, looking like a chocolate covered strawberry."

Shiz turned to take in the rest of the scene, but Jason and Chico pulled the pervert out of the office.

CHAPTER FIFTEEN

A dazzling September afternoon, attracted tourist and Philadelphians, to vibrant South Street. Clothing stores were packed and restaurants were occupied inside and out. Motorist cruised at a snail's pace, looking for somewhere to park or eye candy.

Chip walked along South Street, until he spotted a 'Warnock Art Gallery' sign, which would have caused Chip to be extremely proud, if litter wasn't scattered in front of the establishment. Chip adjusted his tie, tugged on his navy blue blazer, and made his way into the novice operated business.

From the outside of the establishment, Chip could clearly hear Tupac's 'Hit Em Up' classic hit. Chico attempted to greet Chip as he entered the establishment, but Chip kept it moving without a peep. Trash was littered on tables and chairs weren't pushed in. Chip's nostrils flared, as he inched closer to Shiz's concession counter. Shiz greeted his neighbor, but again no response. Chip climbed the stairs to the second floor. The sight of Jason sculpting a cheesesteak, brought a smile upon Chip's face. The presence of someone else startled Jason and sent his three-eighty fumbling from beneath his apron. Eager, not to be hit by a stray bullet, Chip lunge to the left. Jason raced to pick up his strap.

"Chip, what are you doing on the floor?"

"Are you serious?" Chip sounded hysterical.

"What's wrong?" Jason still didn't get the drift.

"Close up, before Johnny Law gets a promotion off y'all two-bit racket." Chip swiftly got to his feet and stormed off towards the stairs. Jason followed the unhappy patron.

As Chip descended to the first floor, he heard Shiz yelling, "Yo ma, you buying or what? Everything must go."

Chip made his way to their only customer, apologized for the gallery closing early, then escorted her to the exit. The open sign on the door, was reversed to closed.

Chico attempted to communicate over the loud music, "Sup OG, why are you shutting us down?"

"First and foremost, turn off that ride or die music. This ain't Sneaker Villa, it's an art gallery." Chico killed the radio, then Chip continued, "I could point out all the flaws in your business, but I'll take it that y'all never been to a successful art gallery before."

Shiz raised his hand. "No, but we can hit the Gallery on Market Street; I'm trying to get the new Yeezy's."

"Shiz, we're talking about you fucking up the churches money and potentially going to jail. This ain't the time to flaunt your vanity." Chip's comment instantly removed Shiz's smile. Chip examined their presentation, then said, "To master any hustle, you must have a reference point to build on. Today, we'll visit some of the top art galleries in Philadelphia, so y'all can have a reference point to build on." Chip turned towards Chico. "Popi, Google the top art galleries in Philly."

In seconds, Chico announced he had Google Maps ready to go. Chip told Jason to put up his apron and firearm, then ordered Shiz to stash the drugs. Once Chip orders were complete, the gallery was secured, and they were on their way.

Mr. Freeman and the Small Business Administration, put Warnock Art Gallery within walking distance of the best art galleries in the city. Once inside their competitors' establishments, Chico took notes and received contact information of talented artist. Jason befriended artist, building on the craft and observing how these seasoned professionals interacted with potential customers. Shiz picked the minds of every attractive woman, followed by asking, "Do you blow tree?".

Upon exiting the last gallery, the group masterminded on ways to improve their enterprise. Chip interrupted them, "So, I'll take it that you have seen the light, like the guy from 'The Allegory of the Cave'."

Jason spoke up first, "I don't think I have ever been in a cave and I have no idea what allegory means, but we're about to take our business to the next level. We need to dim the lights on everything, except our artwork; changing the lighting will magnify the beauty of our artwork and give off a sexy vibe."

Chico followed up, "With Jason's artwork and other artists giving us their art pieces on consignment, we can't lose." Chico nodded his head, envisioning easy money rolling in.

Shiz spoke up next, "We need at least one bad chick working in our establishment. Every art gallery has a bad jawn on staff and I'll be damned if Warnock Art Gallery not known for dimes too. But, those Mofart tracks had me nodding off. We can improve our music, but those Ambien tunes not gonna fly."

"You can play jazz, blues and old school R&B," Chip informed.

"We can do that. Barry White and Marcus Johnson, will have the women open." Shiz rubbed his hands together.

"You know my iPhone is full of panty droppers." Chico tried to high five Shiz.

Shiz inspected Chico's hand. "I don't know why; your palm is the only action you get."

Before Chico could buck at Shiz, Chip jumped in the middle of them. "Don't start, I have something to show y'all." Chip walked away at a rapid pace.

"What'chu talking about Willis?" Shiz mimicked Gary Coleman.

"Don't ask, just follow," Chip instructed.

"I don't have no magnums on me. Do Y'all got any extra rubbers?" Shiz looked at both of his friends, then continued. "Fuck it, I'll just get some sloppy top."

"Fool, I'm not running no train with you." Chip pulled out some keys and with the push of a button, a cocaine white Porsche Cayenne Hybrid came to life. The boys froze.

"I don't ride in Johnnies," Chico told Chip.

"Neither do I," Chip replied, with a shit eating grin.

"Are you telling me, your name is on the registration?" questioned Chico.

"Hell naw, Cherie name is on it."

"You pimping my girl dawg? I should steal you." Shiz stated with vigor. Chip stared into Shiz's eyes and changed his tune. "But, I'm going to let that slide because I feel sorry for y'all ex-cons."

Jason looked puzzled. "I'm confused. You don't hustle anymore, soooo...."

Chip cut him off, "If you think this is a surprise, let's take a ride."

"Now, we getting to the bitches." Shiz speed walked towards the vehicle.

"Bro, we're not busting down no hoes," Chip reminded Shiz.

"Well, let me hold the wheel, so I can?" Shiz put his hand out.

"Young bull, you don't even have a permit," Chip informed his unprepared dreamer.

"Most of the people in Philly don't have a license, but does that stop them from pulling up?" Shiz countered.

"Do you listen to the words that come out your mouth?" asked Chip. Shiz looked up, as if he was trying to figure it out. "Don't answer that, just get in."

Warnock Crew did as told and in no time the Porsche merged into traffic. Chip jumped on Route 76 heading south-west. Jason hyped Chip up, to put the pedal to the floor. Chip smiled before gunning it and sent everyone's head slamming against the headrest. Chip took his foot off the gas, to get off at the Philadelphia Airport exit. Four minutes later, they were at the Philadelphia Auto Bond, in front of 'Chip Cheverly'.

The boys looked at Chip, then the Chip Cheverly sign, at least ten times.

"This is some, Bruce Wayne revealing he's Batman, type shit," interpreted Chico, while inspecting Chip's investment.

"Y'all feeling my dealership or what?" Chip sounded like Mitch from 'Paid in Full'.

"How can you afford this?" Jason asked.

"Now that you're on my level, I'll let you in on my secret. People loved crack in the eighties and I was the plug. Another key was, saving two pennies, out of every dime that touched my hands. Also, Cherie is the true mastermind behind my success, I was just a good worker," Chip admitted. "Let's go check out 'Chip Cheverly'."

Cherie strolled out of the dealership, as they got close to the entrance of the building. A smile came upon her face, as she admired her man with his mentees. "I love watching you mentor those delinquents."

CHAPTER SIXTEEN

Kim and Shiz, strolled hand in hand, down South Street. Kim dawned a red knee length Vera Wing gown and matching Jimmy Choo high heels. Shiz sported a light grey Hugo Boss suit, a pink button up shirt, and wheat brown Johnson and Murphy shoes and belt.

Shiz walked pass the entrance of the art gallery and proceeded to check out his appearance in front of the window front. "Kim, you are fucking with the thoroughest dude in Philly. GQ might recruit a brother tomorrow," he spoke without taking an eye off his reflection.

"Come on big head, you late already." Kim pulled him into the gallery.

The gallery was crammed with art fanatics, consuming water ice and soft pretzels. Teddy Pendergrass's, 'Come on Over to My Place', enticed patrons to hum or sing along. Fabulous paintings, sculptures, and pottery forced patrons to engulf every detail. With the

165

caliber of art given on consignment, on top of Jason's masterpieces, fine art was sold for ungodly prices; and Warnock Art Gallery's Owners took home the lion share of the profit.

Shiz spotted Jason, in his apron, operating the food and fine jewelry stand. The smile on Jason's face indicated that he didn't mind filling in for his tardy companion. Food and fine Jewelry attracts women; plus, Shiz's Persian cashier, Joy, had Jason's head turning often in her direction. Chico on the other hand, did mind the tardiness of his co-worker. With the sophistication of a high end hostess and the smile of a car salesman, who knows he's about to fuck over a potential customer, Chico approached Shiz. Chico leaned in and whispered in Shiz's ear, "Rule number seven, cash before ass."

Shiz stepped back, admired his friend, adjusted Chico's black suit. "It's good for business when Jason is selling merchandise and maybe, Jason will cure his momma's boy issue, interacting with Joy."

Chico grinned harder, as if he was about to have the last laugh, "I wish you could see, what I saw, coming your way."

"Oh, you trying to play a Jedi mind trick on Shiz? Well, Shiz not cracking." Shiz and Chico started a staring contest.

Kim thrusted herself between the two eye doctors. "Hi Chico." Kim strolled seven steps, before the presence of the last laugh, stopped her like an eviction notice.

Shiz crept up behind Kim and attempted to hug her from behind. She smoothly brushed his arms away and speed walked towards her authoritarian father.

"Wow, you're acting brand new today," Shiz looked around to see who observed the diss. "Baby, you know I don't like playing hard to get outside the sack."

"Outside the sack!" Kim's father's eyes almost popped out the socket.

"Ni Hao," Kim greeted her father in Mandarin.

Kim's father folded his arms. "Kill that innocent Chinese girl bit."

As the two began conversing in Mandarin, Shiz wished he had read the subtitles on those Kung Fu movies. But like a kid with A.D.H.D., Shiz quickly lost interest, shrugged and proceeded to walk away.

"You stop now!" Kim's father screamed out, in a tone that would make Chuck Norris shit. Everyone in the gallery, gave him their undivided attention, especially Shiz.

"Kim, can you hold down my stand, while I talk to your pops?" Shiz asked politely. Kim nodded her head in agreement, then he turned his focus toward her guardian, "Sir, can we discuss this issue out back?" The older man nodded his head and Shiz led the way through the crowd.

Kim served over 20 water ices and sold two necklaces, but Shiz and her father were nowhere in sight. Kim asked Joy to hold down the fort, so she could stop the two men from arguing or worse.

As Kim opened the back door, a cloud of indica crashed into her face. "Sean, what are you doing?" She exited the building and slammed the door.

Before Shiz could address the issue, Mr. Wu spoke up. "Hush Kimmy, I used to pinch your weed stash, when mine got low," he said, then proceeded to take a strong pull on the blunt.

Kim mushed her index finger against Shiz's forehead. "Sean, what do you have to say for yourself?"

Shiz smiled, then spoke his mind. "Weed should be legal and thank you. Your dad wants to put my water ice on his dessert menu. Baby, you are my rabbit's foot."

"My restaurant serves rabbit foot, very tender," promoted Mr. Wu.

Kim was at a loss for words, when the back door slammed into her back. Chico exited the gallery and slammed the door behind himself. "Sorry Kim," Chico apologized, then rammed on his partner, "What the fuck Shiz, put out rule number 25."

Shiz formed his hand to imitate someone talking. "Rules, rules, rules."

"Fool, I'm not playing with you," Chico replied.

"Fall back slave driver. I'm celebrating with our new business partner."

"I don't give a damn, if you were celebrating with Jesus, for taking one for the team. Put that shit out," Chico demanded.

Out of nowhere, Chico got hit in the back by the door and Jason came hustling out. "Put out rule 25," Jason yelled with joy. "We just sold my sculpture for thirty racks."

With no rap, Shiz slapped the roach out of Mr. Wu's hand. "You heard…."

Mr. Wu, zipped a karate chop squarely on Shiz's Adam's apple. His chin collapsed to his chest and his knees hit the deck. Kim secured her lover in her arms.

"Sean, you should know, weed and fast reactions no mix. I paranoid, you go down," The elder drop knowledge on Shiz and everyone shared a hearty laugh, except Shiz.

GLOSSARY

a bean- In Philly, we use this line to replace the term one hundred (which means keeping it real) or to tell someone the price is one hundred dollars.

Example: To keep it **a bean** with you, your mom grabbed my ass.

blues- Is slang for Xanax or Xanies.

Example: Those **blues** are the devil, they made me forget my momma's birthday.

bull- Is a word that replaces the name of a person.

Example: The new **bull** on the Sixers, nicer than Iverson (probably not).

cheesesteak- For those of you not from Philly, we do not call cheesesteaks, Philly cheesesteaks in Philly.

Example: A Popi, let me get a **cheesesteak**, with fried onions, pickles, salt, pepper, ketchup, and mayonnaise on the roll. (That's how it goes down in Philly. FYI)

Dipper- A dipper is a cigarette that you smoke, after it has been dipped in embalmed fluid.

Example: I don't know about red bull, but hit a couple **dippers** and you may believe you have wings.

drawlin- The act of doing too much, acting out of pocket, or causing a scene.

Example- I'm goanna to beat your ass, because every time we go out you **drawlin**.

hooyah- This terminology is used in the U.S. Navy, to express excitement for the mission.

Example: We are headed home, **hooyah**!

jawn- Jawn is a word that stands in the place of any noun that comes to mind. Your cousin can be a jawn, your hood can be a jawn, or your car can be a jawn. As you can see a jawn can be a person place or thing.

Example: Stop playing with that **jawn**, before you shoot yourself.

JBM- This acronym is short for Junior Black Mafia. The JBM, was an African American organization, who terrorized every organization in the city of Philadelphia, from the Italian's to Jamaicans. You may have heard their famous saying on the movie 'State Property', "Either, get down or lay down".

Example: You don't want my cousin Ron to come around here, with his **JBM** boys, do you?

make salat/salah- Is a ritual Muslims perform for prayer.

Example: Dawg, how can you **make salat** five times a day, if you hugging the corner 24/7?

NP- Is an acronym for North Philly.

Example: You know NP got the best dope in the city.

ock- This is an Islamic term used when a person is not feeling the other person and don't feel like using their real name.

Example: **Ock**, don't make smack the shit out of you.

ockie or ockies- Is a person or people who practice the Islamic faith.

Example: **Ockie**, you are charging way too much for those oils.

parade rest- Is a military command, that orders the soldier or sailor, to stand with legs shoulders width apart and to place their hands behind their back, with palm in hand.

Example: It's time for uniform inspection, everyone stand at **parade rest**.

Popi Spot- Is a corner store, owned by a person of Latin origin.

Example: Walk me to the **Popi Spot**, so I can grab something to roll this up with.

old head- Is a phrase that you say to an older male, that you have respect for.

Example: **Old head**, the best I can do for you is three for ten.

real rap- Is a line people use before telling the truth or a good lie.

Example: **Real rap**, I woke up with a roach on my lip in her house.

rout- A term we use when we are ready to leave.

Example: This bar is trash, let's **rout**.

Skipper- Is a person who sells wet.

Example: The **Skipper** got that shit, that will have you doing back strokes down the street.

spazzed- To have an angry emotional break down.

Example: You would have **spazzed** out too, if she used all your food stamps, at the beginning of the month.

Septa- A company that owns the trains and buses in Philadelphia.

Example: His stinking ass, got the nerve to be stretched out, on the back of the **Septa** bus.

shot out- This term is used to describe someone who said something crazy or did something off the wall.

Example: You **shot out**, stealing money out of the collection plate.

Thurl- Is a word we use to represent something cool.

Example: That new 760 BMW is **thurl** as shit.

train- We commonly uses this term to replace the word orgy.

Example: I can't believe you grabbed my dick, while running a **train** on that jawn.

tree- This word is used to replace the word weed, marijuana, grass, funk, and every other word used to describe that beautiful plant.

Example: Your weed man, got sticks and seeds in his bags; and I like my **tree** without that mess.

water- This term has nothing to do with H2O. This word, on a Badlands corner, describes PCP, Angel Dust, dead man fluid. And if you don't know, people dip cigarettes or weed in that solution and smoke it to get high. Really High!

Example: I heard they cut their **water** with horse tranquilizer.

wet- Wet is another word for Angel Dust. And I think you get the jest.

Example: That **wet** got me living in slow motion.

wetted- This is a verb for smoking wet or wiggles.

Example: I had to give that fool some milk, to calm down, after getting **wetted** with Marvin.

whomp whomp jokes- Is a corny ass joke someone just said.

Example: Stop serving up those dry **whomp whomp jokes**.

Willie Lump Lump- Is a slang used when someone looks beat up.

Example: You know his mom found out that he stole from her purse and left him looking like **Willy Lump Lump**.

yi mean- Plain and simple, do you understand what I'm saying.

Example: One plus one, equals two, **yi mean**?

young bull- Is a term an older person, would refer to a younger person.

Example: These **young bulls** are robbing anything moving around here.

ABOUT THE AUTHOR

Michael Higgins Jr is a native of Philadelphia, PA. He has gone from a special education student to graduating Summa Cum Laude from the Aviation Institute of Maintenance. He also earned an associate degree in General Education from Prince Georges Community College.

The former U.S. Navy fighter jet mechanic, served two tours overseas, while operating a women's accessories business called D.H. Fashion. Since leaving the U.S. Navy, he has maintained commercial and military aircraft. Aviation contracts have taking Michael Higgins Jr. around the country. He has worked in Tucson, Indianapolis, Beaufort, Fort Drum, and many other aviation hubs to make ends meet.

Currently, Michael Higgins Jr is pre-paring to release his first novel, Warnock Uncut. He lives in Philadelphia and delivers up lifting blogs at www.LaughThinkEat.com.